BIRDWATCHING

A GUIDE TO EUROPEAN BIRDS

by

BERTEL BRUUN

Illustrated by

PHILIPPE DEGRAVE

Consultant for this edition

DEREK WOODS

A LITTLE GUIDE IN COLOUR

PAUL HAMLYN
LONDON · NEW YORK · SYDNEY · TORONTO

FOREWORD

With the increasing interest in birds the demand for books helping in the identification of our feathered friends is great. People travel more than ever; many bird-lovers have the opportunity to visit countries other than their own. It seemed appropriate, therefore, to publish a handy and comprehensive book about European birds, a book whose price makes it accessible to all, and whose size makes it easy to carry along, at home and abroad.

Many ornithologists from all over Europe have been most helpful in the preparation of this book about the more common and widespread species of European birds. We wish to thank in particular Oliver S. Austin, Kai Curry-Lindahl, Erik Hansen, Niels O. Preuss, Chandler S. Robins, Ole Schelde, David C. Seel, Arthur Singer, Francois Vuilleumier, and Herbert S. Zim for their help and suggestions.

B.B.

Pomarine Skua

Published by
THE HAMLYN PUBLISHING GROUP LIMITED
LONDON · NEW YORK · SYDNEY · TORONTO
Hamlyn House, Feltham, Middlesex, England
Copyright © 1967 Western Publishing International
English text Copyright © 1967 Paul Hamlyn Ltd
SBN 601 07967 1
Reprinted 1969
Printed in Italy by Arnoldo Mondadori Editore, Verona

CONTENTS

Blackbird

HOW TO USE THIS BOOK

This book is intended as a pocket guide for the beginner in birdwatching, to be used wherever birds are seen. It was not possible to include all of the birds that can be seen in Europe, and we have limited ourselves to the species that have an extended range and are most frequently seen. Some of the rarer, but more interesting birds are also mentioned in the text. Most of the drawings show the plumage of the male in spring, and if other plumages (winter, female, young's etc.) are shown, this is indicated. Birds are shown in the type of natural surroundings where they are most likely to be observed. The text gives the common name first, then the scientific name of the bird *in italics*. The size indicated in parentheses gives the length in inches from tip of bill to tip of tail when the bird is stretched out. The text describes field characters, voice, and some life history of the bird, as well as, whenever possible, similar or related species that are not illustrated. The maps show the breeding range in red, the wintering range in blue and the areas where these two overlap, where the birds are permanent residents, in purple. The months given for each range indicate the approximate time when the bird can be seen there. The arrows indicate the general directions that are followed in the course of the spring and autumn migrations.

Most of the species descriptions include distribution maps of this type.

4

PARTS OF THE BIRD

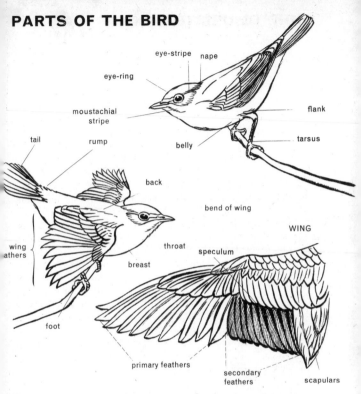

Every scientific subject has its own vocabulary and ornithology is no exception; a technical term is given to nearly all parts of the bird. However only the specialist needs to know the complete vocabulary. It is quite sufficient for the amateur to know only a few technical terms; partly to understand the descriptions he reads and also so that he can describe to his friends or ornithologists birds which he cannot identify. The illustrations above give the names of the main parts of the bird. In this book we have employed as few technical terms as possible.

BIRD CLASSIFICATION

Birds are grouped in orders, each order being divided into families, each family into genera, and each genus into species. Some species are even divided into sub-species. The grouping of birds is primarily based on characteristic structural (mostly internal) similarities. This does not necessarily mean that birds superficially alike belong to the same group. For instance, Divers and Guillemots look alike but do not even belong to the same order. Divers are rather primitive birds developed early in evolution, while Guillemots have developed from gull-like ancestors. As both Divers and Guillemots lead the same type of life (diving and catching fish) they have adapted to surroundings and developed similar traits.

Conversely Gannets and Pelicans, though very different in appearance, belong to the same order. Together with Cormorants, they share the characteristic of having all their toes webbed. But different surroundings and ways of life have led them to develop into very dissimilar birds. When classifying birds, scientists take into account not only structural similarities, but also the origin and evolution of the species. Birds developed from reptile ancestors more than 150 million years ago. The earliest known bird is the Archaeopteryx, found in Bavaria, where it is believed to have lived at least 130 million years ago.

Archaeopteryx

Later many different birds developed and at the time of the last Ice Age more than 10,000 years ago all the European species existed. Today there are about 8,200 species of birds living in the world. These are divided into 27 orders. In Europe about 520 species have been recorded.

CLASSIFICATION OF BIRDS
(European species)

PASSERIFORMES
perching birds

CORACIIFORMES
kingfishers

woodpeckers

PICIFORMES

owls

STRIGIFORMES

nightjars

CAPRIMULGIFORMES

pigeons

COLUMBIFORMES

cuckoos

CUCULIFORMES

CHARADRIIFORMES
waders

birds of prey

FALCONIFORMES

GALLIFORMES
chicken-like birds

PELECANIFORMES
cormorants

grebes

herons

CICONIIFORMES

PODICIPEDIFORMES

ANSERIFORMES
ducks

GAVIIFORMES
divers

Tern   Kingfisher   Diver   Egret

ADAPTIONS OF BIRDS

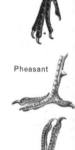

Swallow

Pheasant

Woodpecker

Duck

The feathers, developed from the scaly covering of reptiles, protect the birds from changes in the environment and make flight possible. Further adaptions for flight are internal airsacks and hollow bones, a large heart capable of beating rapidly, and a high metabolic rate.

The shape of the bill often reflects the type of food eaten by a species. Terns, Divers, Herons and Kingfishers all have similarly shaped bills because they all eat fish. In other respects they are very different, as their ways of catching fish vary. Terns dive from the air, Divers pursue fish underwater, Herons patiently stand in the shallow water, and the Kingfisher awaits its prey on a branch above the water. Conversely rather similar looking and closely related birds with different feeding habits may have different types of bill: Shrikes catch large insects, small mammals and birds; the Hawfinch eats hard seeds; the Song Thrush, snails and

Feather

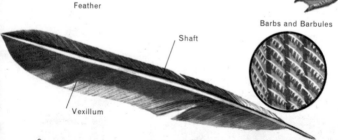

Shaft

Vexillum

Barbs and Barbules

Shrike Bullfinch Thrush Crossbill Warbler

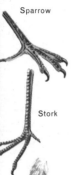

Sparrow

Stork

Owl

Coot

worms; Crossbills cut their way through pine cones to the seeds; and Warblers pick soft insects.

Wings and feet also show characteristic adaptions to the surroundings; the long legs of the Herons, short sturdy feet of Woodpeckers, long elegant wings of the Swifts, and broad wings of the Buzzards, are examples.

Physical and physiological adaptions develop through generations—and thousands of years— but behaviour also adapts itself, and much more rapidly, to the changing world. This is obvious in birds' relations to man: hunted birds are wary, but in areas where there is no hunting, the same birds may be amazingly confident and tame. Another example of changing behaviour is the "domestication" of such birds as Blackbirds and Wood Pigeons. Half a century ago these two birds, now so common in cities and gardens, were found only in woodlands, far from human dwellings.

ng-covert with down

Plumule

Wing-covert

MIGRATION

Not all birds migrate. Some are residents—birds which stay in the same locality all the year round. Others are partial migrants: only a few birds, or only birds breeding in a certain area (usually the northern-most part of the breeding range) moving away from the breeding grounds. Birds are migrants when all, or almost all, of them travel south in the autumn, returning to their nesting grounds in the spring.

It is usually a necessity for the migrants to move south in autumn as most of them live on insects or other food not available in winter in the northern areas where they nest. Many have an inherited urge to migrate long before the shortage of food forces them to do so—most Warblers, for instance. Others (many Ducks) do not move south until forced to do so by cold and ice. What exactly tells the bird when and where to migrate year after year is not known with certainty. Migration is believed to be governed in part by pituitary hormones. Before departure the birds accumulate fat deposits required for the long flights that will bring them to more favourable climates. This internal rhythm is to a large degree governed by the changing light intensity through the year.

Birds "navigate" by the stars and the sun, with the help of an "internal clock", much in the same way as sailors have done for centuries. Recognition of places also plays a role in navigation.

Rock Bunting

Apart from the regular migration from the northern breeding grounds to the southern wintering grounds and back, there are other types of migration, such as the irregular invasions of Crossbills from the north Russian forests. This seems to depend on the production of fir cones on which they feed. The Wall Creeper, living in the high mountains in summer, moves down into the mountain valleys in winter. Some Herons, after nesting and before regular southern migration, spread out in all directions often outside the regions where they are usually seen. Some seabirds (e.g. the Great Shearwater) nesting in the southern hemisphere, spend the winter (which is our summer) on European shores.

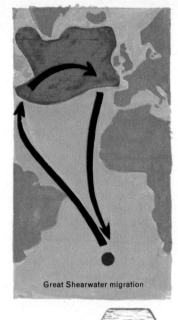

Great Shearwater migration

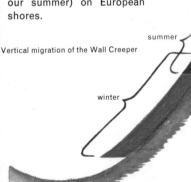

Vertical migration of the Wall Creeper

summer

winter

Many birds migrate at night (most Warblers). Others migrate during the daytime, and some both at night and day. The night migrants can be heard calling in autumn and, particularly, in spring. Birds migrating during the day can easily be observed. Although in the autumn birds fly south over a wide front, there are certain places where they can be seen in particularly large numbers. In the case of the land birds, these places are often along the coasts, which the birds follow instead of crossing the water. On peninsulas pointing in the direction of the migration, such as Falsterbo in Southern Sweden, very large numbers of migrants can be observed in autumn. Another famous locality is the Straits of Bosporus, where thousands of Eagles and Storks pass by. Waterbirds also quite often follow coastlines. When crossing mountains, birds fly through valleys to avoid cold and snow. Areas used for resting during migration are also very favourable for the observation of many different species. Particularly impressive are the numbers of Waders and Ducks congregating in coastal lagoons and river deltas. The Camargue in France is one of the best regions for bird-watching, as well as the Marismas in Spain and the Danube and Volga deltas further east. Of special interest are the islands, such as Fair Isle and Heligoland, where birds are "cast off" when they are thrown off course.

Some of the most important sites for the observation of migrating birds in Europe.

1. Cape Clear 2. Bandsey 3. Skokholm 4. Lundy 5. Slimbridge 6. Spurn Point 7. Gibraltar Point 8. Fair Isle 9. Revtangen 10. Bavandshuk 11. Falsterbo 12. Ottenby 13. Ledskär 14. Signilskär 15. Rubatschi 16. Heligoland 17. Texel 18. Sempach 19. Col des Bretolet 20. Biarritz 21. Camargue 22. Neusidlersee 23. Capri

BIRD RINGING

Birds are ringed around the leg in order to determine when and where they migrate. The method was first practised in 1899 by the Danish schoolteacher Hans Christian Mortensen and since then millions of birds have been ringed all over the world. There are different sizes of rings for different species of bird. Each ring has a number and the address of the ringing station. When the ring is found on the dead bird and returned to the station, the zoologist can tell from the number exactly where and when the bird was ringed. When enough rings have been returned, the zoologist can tell when a certain species migrates, how fast it migrates, what route it follows, the average lifespan of the birds, etc. . . Birds can also be tagged with small labels attached to the wing, or coloured so they can be recognised at a distance. All rings should, of course, be returned to the ringing station when found.

WATCHING BIRDS

Because all birds are interesting and many are very beautiful most people find watching them a pleasurable experience. The pleasure is greater when one knows the birds and their habits. This book will help the beginner—but the most important thing is observing the birds in nature. One can start by watching the birds in one's immediate surroundings, by learning to know the common birds at a glance, studying their characteristics, reading and asking questions about them.

If you have friends who are birdwatchers, they will undoubtedly be more than willing to help. When you know birds that are common in your area, you may begin to look elsewhere, remembering that there are birds in all kinds of surroundings— woods, gardens, fields, marshes, mountains, shores and meadows. The best time to look is early in the morning, when most birds are most active. However many birds can be seen during the day, and at dusk waterbirds and shorebirds are particularly active. At night you can listen to birds singing in spring and summer, and calling during migration in autumn and early spring.

A birdwatcher looks for birds whenever he has the opportunity, no matter what time of the year, because every season has its own characteristic species. If you look out for birds when travelling, you are likely to see many you do not see near your home. When you are out looking, do not rush from place to place. Go slowly and keep your eyes open. Most birds are afraid of humans and will hide or fly away when they see you. You should be quiet and watch, so as to see the birds before they see you. Standing still in one place will usually be more rewarding than dashing about.

It should not be enough to identify a bird. Its habits, movements, flight, song and behaviour, should be observed. If one learns to know each bird as well as one can by watching it, reading about it afterwards becomes more satisfying.

When you want to identify a bird there are certain things you should look for, and one of the secrets of birdwatching is to know exactly what these things are. The size of the bird is important. A Common Gull is very similar to a Herring Gull but is much smaller. Sometimes it is difficult to tell the size of the bird and you should then look for something nearby with which to compare its size, preferably another bird. (In foggy weather birds look bigger than in sunshine). You should also note the shape. A female Mallard and a female Shoveler have approximately the same colours and size, but the shape is very different, the Shoveler having a long broad bill and lying with the breast deeper in the water. Also note the proportions of the bill, head and neck, tail, wings and legs to the rest of the body. Colours are not always easy to see. The light must be good, and often the coloured part you are looking for is hidden (e.g. the speculum of Ducks when not in flight). You should wait for the bird to move, or move yourself.

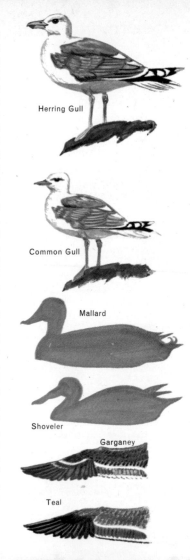

Herring Gull

Common Gull

Mallard

Shoveler

Garganey

Teal

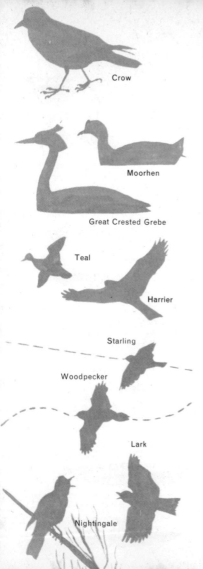

Crow

Moorhen

Great Crested Grebe

Teal

Harrier

Starling

Woodpecker

Lark

Nightingale

Many birds have very characteristic movements. Jackdaws walk on the ground with the head held high, nodding with each step. Warblers are very active, on the move among the branches of trees and bushes. The Wagtails wag their tail, etc... Note these helpful characteristics, also the different ways birds swim: the Grebes effortlessly and gracefully, while a Coot really seems to work for whatever progress it makes. The flight is often characteristic. The Buzzard circles high, hardly moving its broad wings, while the Duck flies straight, beating its pointed wings very fast. When soaring, Buzzards hold their wings straight out from the body, while Harriers hold the tips above the level of the body. Starlings have a straight flight, Woodpeckers an undulating one.

Birds sing, and not only do the songs differ, but also the way they are given. A Nightingale will sing from a bush, a Skylark flying high in the air. Birds also have characteristic calls. These can only be learnt by listening to birds and to recordings.

Although many birds can be seen almost everywhere, most have certain surroundings (habitats) they prefer. In the open sea close to the beaches you will see Divers, Cormorants, Eiders and Scoters on the water, and in the air over them, Gulls and Terns. On the beach itself you will meet the Waders; the species often depends on what kind of beach it is. On sandy beaches, Sanderlings, Ringed Plover and Kentish Plover; on rocky beaches, Turnstones; many more species of Waders congregate on mudflats where much food is to be found.

On inland marshes there are many different Ducks and, often various Waders. Warblers and the Reed Bunting are seen and heard in the reeds. In the meadows and fields Lapwings, Partridges, different Larks and Pipits are found, and in the hedges surrounding open areas, Whitethroats, Buntings and Linnets nest. In winter many birds breeding on the northern tundra, such as Geese, Brambling and Fieldfare, are found in fields. Grebes, Coots, Swans and some Ducks, are found on lakes.

The wood is the home of many species. The birdlife in deciduous and coniferous woods differs, although some species can be found in both. Usually there are fewer species in coniferous woods: the Coal Tit and Crested Tit, Crossbill and Long-eared Owl. Warblers, Thrushes and Woodpeckers are found in deciduous woods, where many Finches and birds of prey also have their home. Most feed in the foliage, but Thrushes and some other species feed on the ground.

Warblers

The woods with the largest number of species are mixed woods with conifers and broad-leaved trees. Parks with bushes and trees, gardens and more open areas also have a large variety of birds; many of these are the same species as found in woods. Even towns, villages and farms have their birds: House Sparrows, Starlings, Swifts, House Martins and Swallows, White Wagtails and Jackdaws. In high mountains, well adapted species like Wall Creeper, Chough, Rock Thrush, Ptarmigan and Alpine Accentor are found. When you see a bird you do not know, you should always note the habitat in which you see it. It is important for its identification.

STUDYING BIRDS

The identification of birds is only a step in the more detailed study of bird biology. A birdwatcher may soon realize how much pleasure can come from studying the birds in detail. In spring the migrating birds begin to arrive singly or in flocks, while the winter guests depart or pass by your area on their way to their northern nesting grounds. Dates should be noted down, as well as the influence of the weather: how cold slows the birds down, how all of a sudden a warm spring day brings many birds while others move north. Then watch the birds in their territory; each male sets up his own and defends it by singing. His song also attracts his future wife. You can observe the pair build their nest, the female lay her eggs, determine

An example of ring recovery. This map shows the places where rings from Coots ringed in Denmark were collected; in red, in summer, and in blue, during the winter.

whether both male and female incubate and follow the young from the time they come out of the eggs until they leave the nest to live a life of their own. Write down the sequence of events, how often the young are fed, and what constitutes their food.

A few birds can be picked out and followed through their breeding season. By putting up nestboxes you can attract several different species for close observation. Nests are also worthwhile studying in detail; the perfectly camouflaged nest of the Chaffinch with its outer shell of lichen and moss and the enormous disorderly pile of branches used year after year by the Buzzard, are interesting examples.

Spring is also the time to study bird songs. Does the bird start singing early in the morning, how long does it continue, and how often does it sing? From where does it sing? A perch in the top of a tree or in the middle of a bush? Usually each species has its own characteristic song habits. Then you can start noting the differences in song between different individuals within the same species. Usually they are small but often you can tell an individual bird by its song and habits.

When the nesting season is over the time for migration begins. Many birds abandon the territories set up in spring and gather in flocks before they depart for more favourable climates. When the migration is under way you can observe it from a good vantage point in the neighbourhood where migrating birds are particularly abundant (some of the best are on coastlines or at the edges of woods) and watch how the species passing by change as the season progresses.

Golden Oriole

EQUIPMENT

The most important equipment for a birdwatcher is a keen eye, a good ear, and a lot of patience. A pair of binoculars can be of great help. Birds are often wary and difficult to approach; binoculars help you watch them from far away. Binoculars should be carefully chosen. The most practical magnification is about X8. Much stronger glasses are not necessarily more helpful, as the field of vision becomes smaller as the magnification increases. Binoculars which admit as much light as possible are the best. The number following the magnification usually indicates the diameter of the lens—the bigger the lens, the more light is admitted. Thus an 8X30 lens admits more light than a lens marked 8X21.

A birdwatcher should always carry a notebook and a pencil. When you see a bird you do not know, write down a description of the size, shape, colour, behaviour and song of the bird, as well as a brief description of the place and circumstances. This will be helpful to identify it later. As you grow more experienced you might want other equipment, such as a field-chair, thigh-waders, etc.... You might also want to pursue special interests, such as photographing birds or recording their songs; this, of course, requires specialized equipment.

ATTRACTING BIRDS

You can attract birds by feeding them. This is particularly rewarding in winter, if snow covers the food birds normally eat. Birds can be fed almost everything left over from the kitchen, or mixed grain sold specially for birds. Food can either be spread on the ground or, better, placed on a special feeding station. Preferably the feeder should have a roof so that the food is not covered with snow, and it should be placed close to a tree or bush so that the birds can seek cover easily. Birds fed in a station can be observed at very close range. Some birds can also be attracted by nestboxes.

The following species will use nestboxes: Kestrel, Stock Dove, Barn Owl, Tawny Owl, Little Owl, some Woodpeckers, Wryneck, all Tits (except Long-tailed and Bearded), Nuthatch, Tree-creepers, Redstarts, Flycatchers, Starling, House Sparrow and Tree Sparrow. The boxes should be designed especially for the species you want to attract; the size and shape of the entrance hole is particularly important. Nestboxes provide birds with nesting sites, which can be scarce in nature, and at the same time the life of the bird during the nesting season can easily be observed. In summer many birds are attracted by birdbaths.

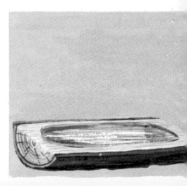

winter

Red-throated Diver

Black-throated Diver

DIVERS (*Gaviiformes*) are large swimming and diving birds with long bodies, rather short necks and pointed bills. In winter they lose their colourful plumage, becoming grey above and white below. They are seen along shores and in large areas of water. The nests, usually with two eggs, are found near the water.

RED-THROATED DIVER (*Gavia stellata*) (23 in.) is the smallest of the Divers. In summer it is recognizable by its red throat. The bill, held slightly upward, is slimmer and more upturned than that of the Black-throated Diver. In winter, when it is often seen in loose flocks along shores, it is more speckled above than the Black-throated Diver.

BLACK-THROATED DIVER (*Gavia arctica*) (25 in.) has a thicker bill than the Red-throated Diver, with

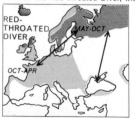

RED-THROATED DIVER
MAY-OCT
OCT-APR

which it often mixes. In summer the back is heavily speckled; but in winter it is uniformly dark grey. As other Divers, it is usually silent in winter but makes yodel-like calls on the breeding grounds. It nests in Northern Scotland, on the Scandinavian Peninsula and along the Baltic, south to Germany. In winter it is found along North Sea and Atlantic coasts, (south as far as Lisbon), on the greater lakes of Central Europe, and the Black Sea. Like the Red-throated Diver, it occasionally appears on reservoirs in Britain.

GREAT NORTHERN DIVER (*Gavia immer*) (30 in.) In summer the neck and head are black with two white-speckled bands on the neck. In winter it is similar to, but much bigger than, the Black-throated Diver. It nests in Iceland and is found in winter further north and further out at sea than the other two Divers.

GREBES (*Podicipediformes*) are medium-sized swimming birds with long thin necks, pointed bills, short tails and individually webbed toes. In summer they are seen on lakes, in winter (when they lose their colourful plumage), mainly along shores or on reservoirs. They are excellent divers. Their barking and wailing yells are only heard on the breeding grounds. The nest floats among reeds.

GREAT CRESTED GREBE (*Podiceps cristatus*) (19 in.) is the largest of the Grebes. During the picturesque courtship two birds approach each other with necks stretched, low over the water, then stand out of the water with the neck in a graceful arch, touching bills. The young (striped black and white) often ride on the back of the swimming parent. In winter, the plumage is dark grey above, white below and the tufts are lost.

RED-NECKED GREBE (*Podiceps grisegena*) (17 in.) is smaller and has a thicker neck. In summer the light-grey cheeks and the red neck identify the bird. It is usually found in smaller lakes than the Great Crested Grebe and leads a more secretive life. It breeds along the Baltic Sea and in Eastern Europe, wintering along the North Sea and the Adriatic coasts.

GREAT CRESTED GREBE

APR-OCT

NOV-MAR

Great Crested Grebes

Great Crested Grebe

Red-necked Grebe

Little Grebe

LITTLE GREBE (*Podiceps ruficollis*) (10 in.) is the smallest of the Grebes. It nests in sheltered ponds and lakes where it leads a very secretive life, often hiding among the reeds, its body submerged with only the head and neck above water. It is slightly paler in colour in winter than in summer. The voice is a characteristic high trill, only heard on the breeding-grounds. When approached, the bird dives rather than flying away.

SLAVONIAN GREBE (*Podiceps auritus*) (13 in.) has a heavier, straight bill. In summer it has golden stripes through the eye, but, unlike the Black-necked Grebe, the neck and sides are chestnut-coloured. It breeds in Scotland and Scandinavia, wintering along Atlantic, North Sea and western Mediterranean coasts and also occasionally on reservoirs.

BLACK-NECKED GREBE (*Podiceps nigricollis*) (12 in.) is unmistakable in summer with its black neck and yellow tufts. In winter it can be told from the Slavonian Grebe by its thin, slightly upturned bill and darker head. It nests in small colonies in sheltered lakes. It usually breeds in Central and Southern Europe, north to the Baltic Sea, and has bred in England and Ireland. It winters along shores and inland waters south of a line from the North Sea to the Bosporus.

Black-necked Grebe

Slavonian Grebe

winter

Manx Shearwater

Fulmar

Storm Petrel

PETRELS AND SHEARWATERS (*Procellariiformes*)

are ocean birds, rarely seen close to land, except after storms and when breeding. Also called Tubenoses (the nostrils form tubes on the upper side of the bill), they are closely related to Albatrosses. They are excellent flyers and all capable of gliding.

STORM PETREL (*Hydrobates pelagicus*) (6 in.) is dark with white upper rump. It flies swallow-like, just above the waves. It nests colonially in burrows on the Atlantic islands from Iceland, south to Northern Spain and on the Western Mediterranean islands.

LEACH'S PETREL (*Oceanodroma leucorrhoa*) (8 in.) is similar, but has a forked tail. It breeds in Iceland, the Faeroe Islands and the islands off the Scottish coast.

MANX SHEARWATER (*Puffinus puffinus*) (14 in.) has a dark upper side, light underside. It nests colonially in burrows and, like the two Petrels, is nocturnal on the breeding-grounds. It flies with very stiff wings, riding the air currents, showing alternately its light underside and dark upper side. It breeds on the Atlantic and Mediterranean islands and along the coasts of England, Scotland, Wales, Ireland, Southern Italy and Greece.

CORY'S SHEARWATER (*Procellaria diomedea*) (18 in.) is a large greyish Shearwater, breeding in the Mediterranean. Outside the breeding season it is also seen in the Atlantic.

FULMAR (*Fulmarus glacialis*) (18 in.) is white, with grey back and upper side of wings. There is also a uniformly grey colour phase. It is heavier and has proportionally shorter wings than the Shearwaters. It often follows ships, flying with stiff wings. It breeds in colonies along the sea-coasts of England, Ireland and Iceland and nests on cliffs.

Cormorant

Gannet

Dalmatian Pelican

Shag

CORMORANTS, GANNETS AND PELICANS
(Pelecaniformes) are large swimming birds, all with four webbed toes. They all nest in colonies and feed on fish: the Cormorant chases them under water, the Gannet dives from great heights, and the Pelican catches them while swimming on the surface.

CORMORANT (*Phalacrocorax carbo*) (36 in.) has a white chin and cheeks. In summer, the breeding birds have a white patch on the thigh. The young bird is dark brown above, light brown below. It is seen along shores and in large lakes. It breeds in colonies in trees, bushes or on cliffs.

SHAG (*Phalacrocorax aristotelis*) (30 in.) is all dark green with no white markings.

GANNET (*Sula bassana*) (36 in.) breeds in colonies on islands above inaccessible cliffs. It is seen elsewhere on coasts in winter.

DALMATIAN PELICAN (*Pelecanus crispus*) (65 in.) nests in the Danube Delta and the Balkans, where it is also found in winter. It is distinguishable from the White Pelican by its grey feet.

WHITE PELICAN (*Pelecanus onocrotalus*) (65 in.) which breeds in Bulgaria and Rumania, has flesh coloured feet and a yellowish tuft.

Purple Heron

Heron

HERONS AND STORKS (*Ciconiiformes*) are large
wading birds with long necks, legs and bills. The
Herons are found along seashores, lakes and rivers.
They nest colonially in trees, bushes or reeds. Their calls
are low-pitched croaks. The Herons fly with their necks
drawn back in an S-shape. Storks, Flamingos, Spoonbills
and Ibises fly with neck outstretched.

GREY HERON (*Ardea cinerea*) (36 in.)
is the biggest and most common
Heron. It is grey with black patterns.
It is often seen fishing among reeds
in rivers, lakes or on sheltered seashores, where it can stand patiently
for hours waiting for a fish to pass
by. It flies with slow wing-beats.

PURPLE HERON (*Ardea purpurea*)
(31 in.) has a similar shape but is
reddish with black and grey markings.
In flight, the neck forms a more open
S than the Grey Heron. It breeds in
Holland, Southern France, Spain,
Italy and the Balkans, wintering in
Africa.

GANNET

GREY
HERON

APR-OCT

Great White Heron

Little Egret

Squacco Heron

GREAT WHITE HERON (*Egretta alba*) (35 in.) is a large, all-white Heron. The bill is dark with a yellow base in summer, and entirely yellow in winter. The feet and legs are dark. It breeds along the lower Danube and in Southern Russia, wintering in Greece and Northern Africa.

LITTLE EGRET (*Egretta garzetta*) (22 in.) is smaller with black bill and legs, and bright yellow feet. It nests in colonies in bushes and swamps, often with other Herons. In summer it is found in Southern Spain, Southern France, Northern Italy and the Balkans, wintering in Greece and Southern Spain.

SQUACCO HERON (*Ardeola ralloidea*) (18 in.) is white with buffish back, head and breast. The legs and bill are greenish. The immature has a darker upper side and dark brown stripes on its breast. It has a shorter neck, and a heavier head and bill than the Little Egret. It breeds in the same area as Little Egret, wintering in Africa.

CATTLE EGRET (*Ardeola ibis*) (20 in.) is all-white in winter. In summer it has light buffish back, crown and breast, and red bill and feet. It is often seen feeding on dry ground, among cattle, eating grasshoppers and other insects. It is found all the year round in Southern Spain and Southern Portugal.

Cattle Egret

BITTERN

APR-OCT

Night Heron
juv.

NIGHT HERON (*Nycticorax nycticorax*) (24 in.) is light grey with black crown and back. The juvenile is dark brown with white spots. It is usually active only at dusk, night and dawn, spending the day hidden in trees or bushes. It breeds along the Mediterranean and the Black Sea, except Greece, wintering in Africa.

BITTERN (*Botaurus stellaris*) (30 in.) active mainly at night, it spends most of the day hidden among reeds. When approached, it often stretches its bill upward, and stands motionless relying on camouflage for protection. The call is a deep, booming "whoomp", similar to the noise made by blowing into a bottle. It nests singly in marshes.

LITTLE BITTERN (*Ixobrychus minutus*) (14 in.) is easily distinguished by its small size. The juveniles look

Bittern

LITTLE BITTERN

APR-OCT

Little Bittern

very much like miniature Bittern. It flies with rapid wing-beats, low over the reeds and is often seen tramping about in reeds. It nests singly in marshes and swamps.

29

White Stork

Black Stork

WHITE STORK (*Ciconia ciconia*) (40 in.) is known to every child. It flies with the neck extended, often soaring very high. It nests on roofs in towns and villages, but also in large free-standing trees. It finds its food (insects, frogs and small rodents)

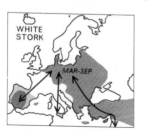

WHITE STORK

MAR-SEP

in marshes or fields, often following harvesting machines. It migrates in flocks. In recent years the numbers of Storks have diminished sharply, in particular in the northern part of its range. The reason for this is unknown but some scientists think it is caused by the extensive use of insecticides against grasshoppers in Africa. When the Storks eat the poisoned grasshoppers, they themselves become poisoned.

BLACK STORK (*Ciconia nigra*) (38 in.) is similar to the White Stork, but has black neck, head and breast. It nests in woods in Eastern Europe and Spain, wintering in Africa. It is more shy and solitary in its habits than the White Stork. It is only rarely seen in Europe outside its breeding range.

FLAMINGO (*Phoenicopterus ruber*) (50 in.) is unmistakable and well-known. It flies with its long neck and legs extended. The wing-beats are fast, interrupted by short gliding. It is often seen in very large flocks. It breeds in large colonies on mud flats. It is found all year round in Southern Spain and Southern France, stragglers being encountered rarely in other parts of Europe.

SPOONBILL (*Platalea leucorodia*) (34 in.) is all-white, with a long flat bill. On the ground it looks very much like a heron. The immature bird is white with black wing-tips. It flies with neck and legs extended. It is usually seen in shallow waters with reedy marshes, where it breeds colonially.

GLOSSY IBIS (*Plegadis falcinellus*) (22 in.) has a long down-curved bill like the curlew, but at a distance it seems almost solid black. It flies with neck and legs outstretched, often with other birds in lines or "V" formation. It breeds colonially in trees or among reeds, along the Lower Danube and the Po Delta, wintering in Africa, occasionally appearing in other parts of Europe particularly in the autumn.

Flamingo

Spoonbill

Glossy Ibis

SPOONBILL

MAR-APR

WATER-FOWL *(Anseriformes)* consist of Swans, Geese and Ducks. (Ducks see p. 35) Swans are large white birds with long necks. Their flight is heavy. The sexes are very similar. They are usually seen on the water. Geese are rather large birds, quite often seen grazing on land. The sexes are similar. They are usually seen in large flocks and like almost all Water-fowl, they often fly in lines or "V"-formation.

im.

Bewick's Swan

Mute Swan

Whooper Swan

MUTE SWAN *(Cygnus olor)* (60 in.) has a red bill with a black knob. Besides its natural range shown on map, it has been introduced in numerous parks all over the world. It builds its huge nest along shores of lakes and sheltered lagoons. The neck is generally held in an "S"-shape and not straight. The young of all Swans are dirty grey in colour ("The Ugly Duckling"). In the flight the wings make a musical throb.

WHOOPER SWAN *(Cygnus cygnus)* (60 in.) has a black bill with yellow base. It usually holds its neck straight. It breeds in northern Scandinavia and Iceland, wintering south to France and the northern Adriatic.

BEWICK'S SWAN *(Cygnus bewickii)* (48 in.) is similar in plumage to Whooper Swan, but has less yellow on bill and is much smaller. It breeds in Arctic Russia, wintering along the North Sea coasts of Great Britain, Holland and Denmark, and in Ireland.

GREY-LAG GOOSE *(Anser anser)* (33 in.) has a big orange bill. In flight the pale forewing is characteristic. It is the ancestor of the Common Farmyard Goose. It seeks its food on fields and in marshes.

BEAN GOOSE *(Anser fabalis)* (32 in.) and the **PINK-FOOTED GOOSE** *(Anser brachyrhynchus)* (28 in.) are closely related. The pink-footed type

nests in Iceland, wintering on southern and western North Sea coasts and in north-western Britain. It is the commonest British Goose in winter. The Bean Goose, which has orange legs, is the most common in Europe.

WHITE-FRONTED GOOSE *(Anser albifrons)* (28 in.) has a white forehead and black bars on the belly. The immature bird has a pink bill without dark markings and lacks the white forehead and black belly. It grazes on fields and marshland.

Grey-lag Goose

Bean Goose

im.

White-fronted Goose

juv.

Lesser White-fronted Goose

Brent Goose

Barnacle Goose

LESSER WHITE-FRONTED GOOSE

(Anser erythropus) (24 in.) is smaller than the White-fronted Goose, the white front extending higher on forehead and with a pronounced white ring around the eye. The immature can be told from the young White-fronted Goose by smaller size, comparatively smaller bill and white eye-ring. It nests in northern Scandinavia, migrating through Eastern Europe to the northern Balkans and Rumania. Stragglers to Western Europe are sometimes seen in flocks of other Geese.

BRENT GOOSE

(Branta bernicla) (23 in.) is almost black, with light belly and rump and a white mark on the sides of the neck. There is also a dark bellied sub-species. The immature birds lack the white neck markings. It is usually seen in flocks along sea-coasts, feeding on eel grass, and only encountered as a rare straggler inland.

BARNACLE GOOSE

(Branta leucopsis) (25 in.) is identified by its black and white markings. It is usually seen along coasts, although it is not as maritime as Brent Goose. It is usually less wary than other geese. It nests in Greenland, Spitzbergen and Novaya Zemlya, wintering in Ireland, Scotland and along the North Sea from Holland to Denmark.

CANADA GOOSE

(Branta canadensis) (38 in.) has a black head and neck contrasting strongly with a white throat patch. The species has been introduced into Great Britain.

DUCKS belong to the order of Water-fowl. Male and female have different plumage, the male being more brightly coloured. Immature birds are similar to females. Surface feeding or Dabbling Ducks (p. 35/39) do not usually dive. They have brightly coloured speculums, which help to identify the dull coloured females and immatures. Diving Ducks (p. 39/42) find their food under water. "Bay Ducks" (p. 40/41) are usually seen in lakes or close to the shore, the larger Diving Ducks (p. 41/42) usually seeking their food at greater depth and further out to sea. Mergansers have toothed bills for holding fish. They are excellent divers, usually seen in lakes or along seashores.

Shelduck
male

im.

SHELDUCK
OCT–APR

SHELDUCK (*Tadorna tadorna*) (24 in.) is a large goose-like Duck with a striking white, black and chestnut plumage. The bill is red; the male's having a large knob. The male is bigger than the female. The immature is white with dark markings, the pattern being more washed-out than that of the adult bird. The wing-beats are slower than most other Ducks. It nests in burrows and under bushes along coasts. The display with a male on the water bowing to a female is often seen. Its voice is a repeated "ack-ack-ack" and a deeper, more drawn-out "ark-ark".

male

female Mallard

male

female

Gadwall

female

female

male

MALLARD (*Anas platyrhynchos*) (22 in.) is the ancestor of the Domestic Duck. It is the most common Dabbling Duck. The glossy green head and mauve breast are characteristic of the male, while the female is distinguished by its mottled brown colour, with a purple speculum. It is found in lakes, swamps and along coasts, where its nest can be found in reeds, grass, under bushes and sometimes in hollow trees. It also lives in parks.

GADWALL (*Anas strepera*) (20 in.) both male and female, are superficially similar to the female Mallard, but are distinguished by their white and brown speculum, conspicuous in flight. The male, even at a distance, looks greyer and has a dark area around the tail. Both male and female have a vermiculated pattern on flanks and sides. It is often seen in flocks with other Dabbling Ducks.

MALLARD

MAR-OCT

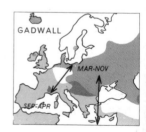

GADWALL

MAR-NOV

SEP-APR

TEAL *(Anas crecca)* (14 in.) is a small Duck with a green speculum. The male has a red head with green and white markings, the female mottled brown, with green and black speculum. It breeds in swamps and near reedy pools. In autumn and winter Teal are often seen in large flocks. The wing-beats are very fast, as is the flight. It usually feeds at dusk and dawn.

GARGANEY *(Anas querquedula)* (15 in.) is only slightly larger than the Teal. The male is recognised by its conspicuous white eye-stripe on the dark head and blue-grey forewing, the mottled brown female by less distinct speculum and light spot at base of bill. Its wing-beats are not as fast as that of the Teal. It is found in very much the same places as the Teal, with which it often mixes, but is usually met in pairs or small flocks.

PINTAIL (*Anas acuta*) (22 in.) has a brown speculum. The male has a brown head and neck, with a white stripe on the side of neck. The tail is very long. The female is mottled brown but has a longer neck and is more slender than the female Mallard. As all Dabbling Ducks, it often reaches the bottom vegetation in shallow water by tipping over, so only the rear end of the body is seen. It nests alongside lakes and on moors and, in winter, is found along coasts.

WIGEON (*Anas penelope*) (18 in.) The male is recognized by the white forewing conspicuous in flight. It has a red head with yellow forehead. The shape of the head is more rounded than that of the Mallard and the bill is much smaller. It nests in moors, ponds and lakes. In winter it is often seen in large flocks along coasts. Sometimes it is seen grazing on land. The voice is a very high characteristic whistle.

Shoveler

Red-crested Pochard

female

female

male

ale

SHOVELER (*Spatula clypeata*)

(20 in.) has a very characteristic long, broad bill. This is used for sifting the water for small insects and plant material, which constitute its food. The male has a greenish-black head, white breast and chestnut coloured belly. The female is mottled brown with a striking blue forewing (which the male also has). When swimming, the front lies very deep in the water. It is mainly seen in marshes, reedy lakes, ponds, and flooded fields where it nests in the reeds or grass.

RED-CRESTED POCHARD

(*Netta rufina*) (22 in.) is, like all the Ducks on the following pages, a Diving Duck, but, unlike most of this group it sits high in the water. The male has a chestnut head, coral-red bill, black breast and white belly with a black stripe through it. The female is dull brown, darker above, lighter below. In flight, both male and female show a conspicuous white band on the wing. It is usually found on large lakes or sheltered lagoons, breeding among the reeds.

SHOVELER

MAR-OCT

DEC-MAR

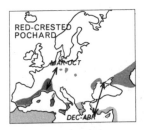

RED-CRESTED POCHARD

MAR-OCT

DEC-APR

39

female

male

Pochard

POCHARD *(Aythya ferina)* (18 in.)
The male has a chestnut coloured
head and black breast; the female is
light brown with grey wing stripes and
indistinct markings around the bill. In
winter it is often seen in flocks with
Tufted Duck. It breeds in reedy lakes
and swamps.

FERRUGINOUS DUCK *(Aythya
nyroca)* (16 in.) is reddish brown
with white under-tail colours. The
male has a white eye. It breeds in
reedy swamps and lakes in Eastern
Europe, Italy and Southern Spain,
wintering in Middle Europe to
Northern Germany and along the
Mediterranean. It is an occasional
visitor to Britain in summer.

TUFTED DUCK *(Aythya fuligula)*
(17 in.) The male is black with a white
belly and has a conspicuous tuft.
Both sexes have a conspicuous
white wingstripe. In winter it is
often seen in very large flocks. It
breeds and winters in the same areas
as the Pochard.

SCAUP *(Aythya marila)* (19 in.) The
male has a black head, neck and
breast and light grey barred back and
belly. The female is brown and has a
conspicuous white ring around the
base of the bill. It breeds along lakes
on the Scandinavian Peninsula and
along the Eastern Baltic Sea. In
winter it is found along the coast of
Northern Europe and Northern
Mediterranean. It is more maritime
in its behaviour than Tufted Duck,
although it is occasionally seen in
flocks with Tufted Ducks.

male

Ferruginous Duck

female

male

Tufted Duck

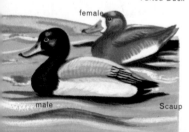

female

male

Scaup

POCHARD

APR-NOV

OCT-APR

WHITE-HEADED DUCK (*Oxyura leucocephala*) (18 in.) is a Diving Duck with a large head and a long pointed tail. When swimming it lies deep in the water with the tail cocked almost vertically. The male has a white head and a pale blue bill. It is a resident of Southern Spain and Italy and a summer visitor to the Lower Danube.

GOLDENEYE (*Bucephala clangula*) (18 in.) has a dark head, the male with a white spot in front of the eye, white breast and underside, and characteristic square white wing patches. The flight is far noisier than any other duck. Its nest is found in burrows, hollow trees or hidden under bushes close to lakes, rivers and the seashore. In winter it is mainly seen in small flocks, along coasts, or larger lakes.

LONG-TAILED DUCK (*Clangula hyemalis*) (21 in.; tail-feathers of male included) is characteristically white and black. In winter it is found in flocks along sea-coasts usually rather far out. The flight is very fast. It is the most maritime of the ducks. It is very noisy, the male having a nasal whistle, the female a more barking note. It nests in Northern Scandinavia and Iceland, wintering in the Baltic, North Sea and northern-most Atlantic, south to Brittany.

White-headed Duck

female

male

Goldeneye

female

male

Long-tailed Duck

winter

winter

female

male

summer

Common Scoter

male   female

Velvet Scoter

male   female

Eider

male   female

COMMON SCOTER *(Melanitta nigra)* (19 in.) is a medium-sized all black Diving Duck. The male has a partly yellow bill. The female is dark brown with white cheeks. It nests near lakes and seashores and is in winter found along coasts and occasionally inland waters in flocks, often mixed with Velvet Scoters. The compact build and lack of white on the wing distinguish it from the Velvet Scoter.

COMMON SCOTER — MAY-SEP — SEP-APRIL

VELVET SCOTER *(Melanitta fusca)* (22 in.) is black with a distinct white wing-band. In winter it is usually found along sea-coasts. It breeds on the Scandinavian Peninsula and along the Baltic Sea, wintering along the Atlantic coasts from Northern Norway south to the Bay of Biscay.

EIDER *(Somateria mollissima)* (23 in.) is the biggest of the Diving Ducks. The male is white with black markings, the female is mottled brown. It is seen along coasts, sometimes mixing with Scoters. It flies in long lines low over the water. It breeds and winters along the coasts of Northern Europe, south to Normandy. On the breeding grounds, the down is collected from the nests for use in pillows and eiderdowns.

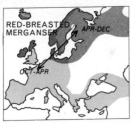

RED-BREASTED MERGANSER APR-DEC OCT-APR

RED-BREASTED MERGANSER
(*Mergus serrator*) (23 in.) is the most
common of the Mergansers. These
have long slender bills with ragged
edges (for holding fish) and long
slender bodies. They are all excellent
divers. The male of the Red-breasted
Merganser has a characteristic crest
and a brown breast-band. It is mainly
found along coasts, nesting under
bushes and amongst rocks.

GOOSANDER (*Mergus merganser*)
(26 in.) is the largest Merganser. The
male has a greenish-black head and
salmon coloured underside. The
female is very similar to the female
Red-breasted Merganser, but has a
more clearly defined white throat
band. The build is also heavier. It
nests in hollow trees.

SMEW (*Mergus albellus*) (16 in.) is
the smallest Merganser. The male is
white, with black lines. The female
has a conspicuous chestnut cap. The
bill is comparatively short. It nests
in hollow trees in northern Scandinavia and Russia, wintering south to
the Mediterranean. Unlike the Red-
breasted Merganser, Goosander and
Smew are usually found on large
areas of fresh water in winter.

GOOSANDER MAR-NOV OCT-APR

Red-breasted Merganser

male female

Goosander

male female

Smew

male female

BIRDS OF PREY *(Falconiformes)* have strongly hooked bills and powerful feet with long curved claws. The Eagles and Vultures are the biggest of this group. The majority of birds of prey are usually seen soaring but Accipters, Harriers and some Falcons only rarely do so. Many large birds of prey live partly on carrion; the Vultures do so almost entirely. The smaller ones almost invariably catch live prey. The nests are very variable and can be huge structures of sticks weighing several hundredweight. They are usually made in trees, rock ledges, on the ground or in the old nests of other birds. Generally the larger species only lay one or two eggs, the smaller types often laying several. The eggs are usually white, blotched with reddish brown.

Griffon Vulture

Bearded Vulture

Black Vulture

Egyptian Vulture

EGYPTIAN VULTURE *(Neophron perenopterus)* (25 in.) is the smallest and most common of the Vultures. The white plumage and black wing tips make it easy to identify. Immature birds are dark brown. It is often found near towns and villages, living mainly on refuse. It is a resident of the Iberian and Balkan Peninsulas and Mediterranean coasts.

BLACK VULTURE *(Aegypius monachus)* (40 in.) is dark brown with a brown ruff. It is a resident of Spain, Portugal, the Mediterranean Islands, Balkans, and the Black Sea coast.

BEARDED VULTURE *(Gypaetus barbatus)* (43 in.) has very long, comparatively narrow wings and tail. It is mainly seen in mountain areas. It is a resident of Spain, the Mediterranean Islands and Greece.

GRIFFON VULTURE *(Gyps fulvus)* (39 in.) is brownish with a whitish ruff. The tail is very short. Although it can be found in all kinds of habitat, it has a preference for mountainous areas.

GOLDEN EAGLE (*Aquila chrysaetos*) (34 in.) is the most widespread of the Eagles. It has a majestic flight. The adult is uniformly dark brown with a golden hind neck. The immature bird is uniformly dark with a distinct white patch on the wing and a white tail with broad black terminal band. It nests in mountains. It hunts hares and larger birds, but will often be found eating carrion. In spite of tales it is generally harmless to sheep and cattle.

GOLDEN EAGLE

Golden Eagle

IMPERIAL EAGLE (*Aquila heliaca*) (32 in.) has white scapulars; the Spanish form also has a conspicuous white fore-wing. The immatures are mottled brown. It is a resident of the southern Iberian Peninsula, Rumania, Bulgaria, Northern Greece and Eastern Jugoslavia. It prefers open country but sometimes nests in forests.

Imperial Eagle

LESSER SPOTTED EAGLE (*Aquila pomarina*) (25 in.) is dark brown. The immatures have a few white spots on the upper-side of the wing and a small rusty patch on the hind neck. It nests in Eastern Europe from the Baltic south to the Mediterranean, wintering along the Eastern Mediterranean. It prefers damp wooded country.

Lesser Spotted Eagle

White-tailed Eagle

im.

Bonelli's Eagle

Booted Eagle

Short-toed Eagle

WHITE-TAILED EAGLE *(Haliaeetus albicilla)* (34 in.) is brown, the adults with a pure white tail and yellow bill. The immature bird is dark brown. The flight is often laborious and very heavy. The tail is short and the neck long. It is found mainly along shores of lakes and seas where it eats dead fish washed ashore, and an occasional bird. It nests in trees or cliffs.

BONELLI'S EAGLE *(Hieraaetus fasciatus)* (28 in.) has a white underside streaked with black, with dark wings and a black band on the tail. It is a resident of the mountainous regions of Spain and Southern France, Southern Italy and Greece.

BOOTED EAGLE *(Hieraaetus pennatus)* (20 in.) has a whitish underside with a long unmarked tail. There is also a dark phase. It breeds in the woods of the Iberian Peninsula and South-eastern Europe west to the Adriatic, wintering in Africa.

SHORT-TOED EAGLE *(Circaetus gallicus)* (26 in.) is white below with dark upper breast and a long barred tail. It is a summer visitor to South-western Europe, north to Central France, and to South-eastern Europe north to the Baltic. Some remain in South-western Europe in winter.

Buzzard

Rough-legged Buzzard

BUZZARD *(Buteo buteo)* (21 in.) is one of the most common of the Birds of Prey. It varies much in coloration but the general pattern, with the dark breast band, is fairly constant, although whitish birds can be seen. It nests in trees and on cliffs and rocks. It lives mainly on rodents and does very little harm to game birds and poultry. It will often be seen on a branch, sitting absolutely still on the look-out for prey.

ROUGH-LEGGED BUZZARD *(Buteo lagopus)* (24 in.) resembles the

Buzzard, but has a mainly white tail with a broad dark band at the end and generally a pale head. The dark breast band is situated lower than that of the Buzzard. The legs are feathered to the toes, but this cannot be seen in the field. It is often seen hovering over fields when it is hunting mice, and like the Buzzard it is often seen perched on poles. It nests on mountains in Scandinavia, migrating south in winter where it prefers open country, marshes and farmland. Even in winter it is not as common as the Buzzard.

BUZZARD

MAR-OCT

ROUGH-LEGGED BUZZARD

MAR-NOV

OCT-APR

Sparrow Hawk
male
female

male
female

Goshawk

SPARROW HAWK *(Accipiter nisus)* (13 in.) is a rather small long-tailed Bird of Prey, with broad but short wings. The flight is fast and the wing-beats strong. As in the case with many Birds of Prey, the female is bigger than the male. It nests in trees in woods. It hunts smaller birds at the edges of the woods and along hedgerows. It is only rarely seen soaring. It is one of the most common Birds of Prey.

SPARROW HAWK

GOSHAWK *(Accipiter gentilis)* (22 in.) has a plumage similar to the Sparrow Hawk, but is much bigger. The under-tail coverts form a white fluffy patch. It has a much heavier flight than the Sparrow Hawk. It nests in woods. Its habits are very secretive and it usually keeps out of sight among trees. It is less often seen than the Sparrow Hawk and will kill a wide range of medium-sized birds and mammals.

KITE

KITE *(Milvus milvus)* (24 in.) has a long forked tail. The plumage is reddish. It nests in trees in woods and hunts its prey (rodents and birds) in woods and on open fields. It also eats carrion.

BLACK KITE *(Milvus migrans)* (22 in.) is more common than the Kite, is darker and has a less forked tail. It is often seen over lakes and rivers, where it takes fish from the water and also feeds on dead fish and similar carrion. Sometimes seen in flocks. It breeds in the same parts of Europe as the Kite, except Wales, Corsica and Sardinia, migrating to Africa in winter.

HONEY BUZZARD *(Pernis apivorus)* (22 in.) looks very much like a Buzzard, but is known from this by its kite-like style of flight and its longer, more heavily banded tail. It nests in trees in woods. The main food is wasps, their nests and larvae, which it digs out of the ground. The feathers of the face are shaped to protect it from the stings of the wasps. On migration, it is may be seen in flocks with Buzzards.

HONEY BUZZARD

APR-SEP

Kite

Black Kite

Honey Buzzard

female

male

Marsh Harrier

Hen Harrier

male

Montagu's Harrier

male

male

MARSH HARRIER (*Circus aeruginosus*) (21 in.) is the heaviest and darkest of the Harriers. In flight, the wings are held with tips pointing upwards, forming a "V" like other Harriers. It is usually seen over or near reeds, where it nests. Its food consists of rodents, frogs and birds.

HEN HARRIER (*Circus cyaneus*) (19 in.) has a distinct white rump; the grey-blue male is clear white below the breast and has black wing-tips. The immature resembles the brown female. It nests in moorland. In winter it is also seen in other types of open country, over fields and marshes.

MONTAGU'S HARRIER (*Circus pygargus*) (17 in.) also has a white upper-rump, but the male can be told by black stripes on the wing. The immature is reddish brown. The female is almost identical to the female Hen Harrier. It breeds in England and Continental Europe south of the Baltic, migrating to Africa in winter.

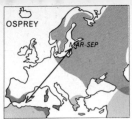

OSPREY *(Pandion haliaetus)* (23 in.) is white below, with a distinct breast band and dark above with a white crown. The wings are long and held at an angle. It nests in trees near open water, where it catches fish by plunging into the water feet first. The prey is carried away in the claws. Fish up to four pounds in weight have been recorded taken by Ospreys. When feeding, it will often be seen standing still at the same spot over the water, hovering, but usually flies with alternating flapping and gliding.

PEREGRINE FALCON *(Falco peregrinus)* (18 in.) is used by falconners to catch pigeons and other birds. It has a barred under-side and dark upper-side and a characteristic stripe on the side of the head ("moustache"). The flight is strong and fast and in a dive it can attain a speed of 200 m.p.h., although in regular straight flight it only does about 40 m.p.h. It nests in trees or on cliffs. The food consists of birds (pigeons, ducks, shorebirds) caught in the air.

GYR FALCON *(Falco rusticolus)* (22 in.) is the most spectacular European bird of prey. It has two colour phases; white and grey. The flight is even faster than the Peregrine and the Gyr looks broader-winged in flight. It breeds in Iceland and Scandinavia and occurs occasionally in Britain in winter.

Osprey

Peregrine Falcon

Hobby

HOBBY

APR-SEP

HOBBY *(Falco subbuteo)* (13 in.) looks like a small Peregrine Falcon, but has reddish brown thighs. It nests in open woods. It catches small birds in flight, and can even capture swallows and swifts. In autumn it migrates to Africa. In flight it resembles a large swift.

MERLIN *(Falco columbarius)* (12 in.) has more indistinct markings, the male being dark-bluish above, brownish streaked below, without the characteristic "moustache". The female is brown above. It nests on the ground and sometimes in old nests in trees. It hunts small birds, low over the ground, and has a swift, strong flight.

RED-FOOTED FALCON *(Falco vespertinus)* (12 in.) male is almost black, with red thighs and under-tail coverts. The female is light orange-brown. It lives mainly on insects caught in flight. It is a summer visitor to South-eastern Europe (not Greece), wintering in Africa. It occasionally wanders to England and Northern Europe.

female

Merlin

male

Red-footed Falcon

female

male

MERLIN

MAR-OCT

SEP-APR

Kestrel

male

female

Lesser Kestrel

KESTREL *(Falco tinnunculus)* (13 in.) is the most common of the Falcons. The male has a blue head and tail, red back spotted with black and black wing-tips. The female is reddish brown above, streaked below. The immatures are similar to the female. It nests in trees (often using the abandoned nests of other birds such as crows or buzzards), on cliffs, and even in buildings like barns and churches. It lives mainly on insects and rodents caught on the ground. When hunting, it will often stand still in the air, hovering. It is often seen sitting on telephone wires or poles.

LESSER KESTREL *(Falco naumanni)* (12 in.) has a plumage almost identical to that of the Kestrel. The male can be told from the Kestrel male by having unspotted upper part. The claws are white, whereas those of the Kestrel are black. It is often seen in towns and villages, nesting in old buildings, ruins, barns etc. It is much more gregarious than the Kestrel and large flocks are often seen. In behaviour and hunting, it is similar to the Kestrel. Unlike most other birds of prey, its voice is often heard. The most common note heard is a repeated "che-che-che-che".

KESTREL

MAR-OCT

LESSER KESTREL

MAR-SEP

GALLINACEOUS BIRDS (*Galliformes*) are land birds closely related to the domestic chicken. The bills are short and stout, the feet heavy and strong, used for scratching in the ground for food. The hind toe is short and usually raised above the other toes. The wings are comparatively short and have stiff feathers, the flight being laborious with very fast wing-beats.

BLACK GROUSE (*Lyrurus tetrix*) (female 16 in., male 25 in.) is found in heaths, plantations, openings in woods and similar places. The male has a lyre-shaped tail. The female is mottled brown, with a slightly forked tail. In early Spring the males gather in special places where they make their display and fight. The tail is raised vertically, the plumage is puffed up, and the wings hang down. They make a cooing sound when fighting over the females. During this display, the birds can be approached quite easily, but outside the season they are wary.

Capercaillie

Black Grouse

CAPERCAILLIE (*Tetrao urogallus*) (female 24 in., male 34 in.) is the biggest of the European Chicken-like Birds. The male is black, but the tail is fan-shaped. It, too, has special places where the display is performed. It is found in coniferous woods, mainly in the mountainous parts of Europe. Hybrids between the Capercaillie and the Black Grouse are not uncommon.

BLACK GROUSE

CAPERCAILLIE

Willow Grouse

(not brown). Its habits are similar to Willow Grouse. It is resident in the mountains of Scandinavia, Scotland, Iceland, the Pyrenees and the Alps.

RED GROUSE (*Lagopus scoticus*) (15 in.) is very similar to Willow Grouse and Ptarmigan, but is brown all year round and has brown wings. The colour of the male is more reddish-brown than that of the female. It is resident on moorland throughout Britain.

Hazel Hen

WILLOW GROUSE (*Lagopus lagopus*) (16 in.) is, in winter, white with a black tail. In summer the body is brown, the wings white. In winter it can be told from the Ptarmigan by the bigger bill and lack of a black stripe from bill to eye. It is found in heaths and moors of primarily mountainous areas. It is often seen in small flocks. When flushed, it will often look back over the wing while in flight.

PTARMIGAN (*Lagopus mutus*) (14 in.) is similar to Willow Grouse in winter, except for the male having a black stripe between the bill and eye. In summer the male has a grey body

HAZEL HEN (*Tetrastes bonasia*) (14 in.) has black band on tail and the male has a black throat bordered with white. It is found in woodlands and often perches in trees.

WILLOW GROUSE

HAZEL HEN

Partridge

Red-legged Partridge

Rock Partri[dge]

PARTRIDGE (*Perdix perdix*) (12 in.) has a brown face and upper-side, grey breast and dark brown spot on the belly. It is common in farmland and in open pastures, where it nests. It lays up to 20 eggs. In winter, families stick together in flocks of 10—15 birds. It is a valuable game bird.

PARTRIDGE

RED-LEGGED PARTRIDGE (*Alectoris rufa*) (14 in.) is found in drier and more rocky locations than the Partridge. It is resident in England, France and the Iberian Peninsula. It is very similar to the Partridge, but has a white throat bordered with black stripes and a reddish belly, tail and feet. It is a more restless bird than the Partridge and its movements are quicker. It will often take flight by running, rather than flying. The display note is a characteristic "chucka chucka".

ROCK PARTRIDGE (*Alectoris graeca*) (14 in.) is similar to Red-legged Partridge, except that the white throat is bordered with solid black. It is a resident of the Alps, in Italy and the Balkan Peninsula. It is, in habit, similar to the Red-legged Partridge with even more preference for stony and rocky areas.

QUAIL (*Coturnix coturnix*) (7 in.) is streaked brown. It nests in fields and grasslands. In spring, the characteristic three-toned whistle of the male is given by day and by night. Contrary to other European Gallinaceous birds, it migrates, doing so at night. It winters in Africa. The numbers present fluctuate greatly from year to year. It is quite rare in its northward distribution.

QUAIL

APR-DEC

PHEASANT (*Phasianus colchicus*) (female 24 in., male 34 in.) with its beautiful colours and long pointed tail, is well known. The female is mottled brown with a pointed tail. It was originally introduced into Europe as a game bird, and although most are now completely wild, a large number of chicks are released every year. It thrives in fields, parkland and open woods, but can be met with almost anywhere within its range.

PHEASANT

Quail

Pheasant

female

male

CRANES AND RAILS (Gruiformes) are marsh birds of various sizes. The Cranes are among the largest and most beautiful of all birds. Different species are found almost all over the world; some of them threatened by extinction like the Whooping Crane of North America and the Manchurian Crane found in the Far East. Rails are rather secretive birds, more often heard than seen. They are almost all marsh birds. Coots and Moorhens are plump birds with long toes, found more in the open.

Crane

CRANE (Grus grus) (45 in.) is a large stork-like bird. It is dark grey with black head and neck, a white stripe going down on the side of the neck, and a red crown. The inner secondaries are extended, forming the fluffy "tail". It flies with the neck extended, slow, strong wing-beats and, during migration, often in "V"-formations or lines. On the ground it walks slowly and gracefully and, in spring, a picturesque dance, consisting of jumps and bows, is performed. It breeds in swampy areas and in winter is usually seen on open fields and moors.

CRANE

MAR-OCT

OCT-MAR

WATER RAIL (*Rallus aquaticus*) (11 in.) is a long-billed dark bird. It is usually only heard, as it stays hidden in dense reeds in swamps or along rivers. It has a large variety of noises, which are sometimes compared to those of a pig in distress. It is most often heard at night. The nest is situated among reeds. It is probably the most common of the Rails and also the least secretive in its habits.

SPOTTED CRAKE (*Porzana porzana*) (9 in.) has a short bill, but its habits are similar to those of the Water Rail, although it is more secretive. It often frequents smaller areas of water than the Water Rail. The voice is a repeated whistle similar to the noise made by the fast striking of a thin stick. When it is nervous, the short tail is cocked and flicked at each step.

Baillon's Crake

Little Crake

to Eastern Europe, west to West Germany, south to Northern Italy and Greece, and north to the Baltic.

CORNCRAKE *(Crex crex)* (11 in.) has a dull yellowish colour and a short heavy bill. When it is flushed, (which is difficult) a chestnut patch on the wing is characteristic. It nests in fields, pastures and meadows. In spring and early summer, the male calls both by night and by day. The call is a rasping and penetrating "arp-arp". It has been compared to the noise made when you run a nail over the teeth of a comb. The bird is not often seen, as it hides in the lush vegetation. It migrates at night.

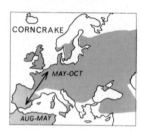

CORNCRAKE

MAY-OCT

AUG-MAY

BAILLON'S CRAKE *(Porzana pusilla)* (7 in.) has a brown upper-side, bluish-grey throat and breast, and barred blackish and white belly and flanks. The sexes are similar. It is found in marshes and pools with dense vegetation. It is a summer visitor to Portugal, Spain, France Northern Italy and the Lower Danube area.

LITTLE CRAKE *(Porzana parva)* (7 in.) male is very similar to Baillon's Crake, but lacks the barred belly and flanks. The female is buffish brown on the underside. It nests in swamps and marshes. It is a summer visitor

Corncrake

Coot

Moorhen

COOT (*Fulica atra*) (15 in.) is all black, with a white shield over the white bill. The legs and feet are greenish with individually webbed toes. It nests in lakes, on reedy shores of sheltered bays and swamps. In winter it often gathers in large flocks, mixing with Tufted Ducks and other Diving Ducks. It is then often seen in salt water (lagoons and bays).

MOORHEN (*Gallinula chloropus*) (13 in.) is black with white under-tail coverts and a red shield over the bill. The legs are long, as are the toes. The immatures are greyish, darker above and lighter below. It nests in ponds, along streams and in swamps, most often seen along the edge of the reeds. When suspicious, it cocks its tail and jerks it up and down.

COOT APR-NOV

MOORHEN APR-OCT

BUSTARDS *(Otididae)* are large steppe birds. They are also found on cultivated fields. They have rather long legs, long necks and a strong, medium-length bill. They are usually quite wary. They did have a much larger distribution in Europe than they have today and their decline has been caused mostly by hunting. In flight they keep their head and feet outstetched.

Great Bustard

Little Bustard

GREAT BUSTARD *(Otis tarda)* (male 40 in., female 30 in.) has a grey neck and head and under-side, brown upper-side and large white patches on the wing, distinctive in flight. The flight is very fast with regular beats of the very broad wings. It is often seen in small flocks. It is a bird of the open plains and nests on the ground. It is very shy and wary and difficult to approach.

GREAT BUSTARD

LITTLE BUSTARD *(Otis tetrax)* (17 in.) is brown above and whitish underneath. It, too, has a large amount of white on the wing. The male has a black neck with white bands. It is found in open grassland and larger fields. When approached, it will often crouch instead of escaping by taking flight. When flying, the wing-beats are much faster than those of the Great Bustard.

LITTLE BUSTARD

WADERS *(Charadriiformes)* This order is divided into three groups—Waders *(Charadrii)*; Gulls, including Skuas and Terns, *(Lari)*, and Auks *(Alcae)*. Waders have rather pointed wings; the sexes are usually similar. The nests are usually on the ground, the eggs spotted and difficult to see. The young leave the nest immediately after coming out of the egg. Oystercatchers are large Waders with long, strong bills. Stints and Avocets are quite large, with long bills and extremely long legs. Plovers are small to medium-sized, rather compact birds; there are two groups, the smaller ones (ringed) and the larger ones (not ringed). Turnstones are compact and short-billed, short-legged and long-winged. Curlews are big, long-legged, dull coloured with very long down-curved bills. Godwits have straight or upturned bills. The Sandpipers are medium-sized, slim, rather long-legged and long-billed. The smaller Sandpipers ("peeps") are small and short-legged, usually seen in large compact flocks. Woodcocks and Snipes are very characteristic with very long bills, short legs and plump bodies. Phalaropes superficially resemble the small Sandpipers, but have individually webbed toes and swim very well.

eggs

chicks

Lapwing

Oystercatcher

Avocet

Lapwing

Oystercatcher

Lapwing

OYSTERCATCHER *(Haematopus ostralegus)* (17 in.) has a black head, neck, breast and back, white belly and white wing-stripe and a characteristic long orange beak. It nests on seashores and, in the northern part of its range, also inland. In winter and on migration, it is seen in shallow water along coasts. It feeds on snails, molluscs and worms, by poking its bill into the ground. It migrates in flocks along seashores. The voice is a shrill "kleep" and often heard.

LAPWING *(Vanellus vanellus)* (12 in.) has a metallic black back, black throat and front of breast, white belly and the long black crest. The wings are long, broad and rounded. At the breeding ground the flight is acrobatic but when migrating in flocks, it is straight with regular wing-beats. It nests in open meadows and fields and is, in winter, found along shores and on fields. In early autumn, the Lapwings gather in large flocks before migrating. The voice is a characteristic "kee-vit". It is one of the most common waders.

OYSTER-
CATCHER   FEB-OCT

LAPWING

FEB-OCT

OCT-APR

RINGED PLOVER *(Charadrius hiaticula)* (7 in.) is a small Wader with a light brown back, white underside and a white ring, bordered with black, around the neck. The legs are orange and the bill is orange with a black tip. It nests along seashores, sometimes inland. In flight, a distinct wing-stripe is seen. It runs very fast, almost rolling along the beach, with sudden stops when it stands completely still.

RINGED PLOVER

MAR-OCT

AUG-JUNE

Ringed Plover

Little Ringed Plover

Kentish Plover

LITTLE RINGED PLOVER *(Charadrius dubius)* (6 in.) is quite similar, but has no wing-stripe and the legs are flesh coloured. It also has a white stripe above the eye. It prefers fresh water and is often found nesting in old gravel pits. It is a summer visitor to all of Europe, except Northern Scandinavia, Scotland and Ireland, wintering in Africa and along the Mediterranean.

KENTISH PLOVER *(Charadrius alexandrinus)* (7 in.) is lighter in colour. It does not have a black band on the breast and the feet are black. It is seen on sandy beaches, nesting along the coast of Europe, north to Scandinavia, and winters along the southern parts of the Mediterranean coasts.

GREY PLOVER (*Pluvialis squatarola*) (11 in.) is grey above, white below in winter, black below in summer. In flight, it can be told from Golden Plover by having a black patch on the underside of the wing. In winter, it is found along seashores, often alone or in small, rather loose flocks. It is a rather shy and wary bird. The flight call is a high-pitched and rather sad-sounding trisyllabic "tlee-oo-ee". It lives on worms, insects and snails that it picks up on the mud flats.

GOLDEN PLOVER (*Pluvialis apricaria*) (11 in.) is mottled gold and black above and light below in winter, black below in summer. The sub-species, breeding in Northern Germany and England, has less black on breast and throat. It nests on open moors and heaths and in winter is found in fields and meadows in large flocks. Golden Plovers will often fly in "V"-formation or long lines. The voice is a clear whistle.

TURNSTONE *(Arenaria interpres)*
(9 in.) is a long-winged short-legged and short-billed Wader. In summer, it has a rusty back with distinct black and white markings and the characteristic face pattern of black and white. In winter, the back and face are more dusky and less colourful. It is usually seen along seashores, where it seeks its food (insects, worms and snails) between the rocks and in the seaweed. Its name is derived from the habit of turning stones to look for food underneath. The voice is a staccato "tuk-a-tuk".

TURNSTONE
AUG-MAY

DOTTEREL *(Eudromias morinellus)*
(8 in.) looks like a small golden plover. It has a darker upperside and a distinct white eye stripe. The breast is grey, the underside chestnut coloured. The male is not as beautifully coloured as the female and it is also smaller. The male also takes care of incubation and, later, of the young. It breeds in mountains, in winter being seen on moors and fields. It is a very tame bird.

DOTTEREL
MAY-SEP
OCT-MAR

summer
winter
summer
Turnstone

SNIPE (*Gallinago gallinago*) (11 in.) is chunky, long-billed and short-legged. The general colour is brown, dark above, whitish below. It has three stripes on the head and white borders on the tail. It is often seen in small flocks, flying to the feeding grounds in the evening. When displaying in flight, its tail feathers make a buzzing sound. When flushed, it will fly away in a zig-zag pattern. It is found in wet bogs, marshes and swamps.

JACK SNIPE (*Lymnocryptes minimus*) (8 in.) has four stripes on the head and no white on the tail. It is usually seen singly and is harder to flush than the Snipe. Its flight is also slower and not as zig-zagging. It usually throws itself on to the ground after a short flight. It occurs in the same habitat as the Snipe.

Great Snipe

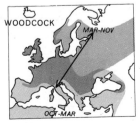

GREAT SNIPE *(Gallinago media)* (11 in., of which the bill is about 2½ in.) is larger and heavier than the Snipe. The tail is bordered with white. The underside is more barred and the body in general gives the impression of being more barred than the Snipe. The flight is rather slow and direct, without zig-zagging. It is usually found on dryer ground than the Snipe. The numbers have diminished rapidly during this century.

WOODCOCK *(Scolopax rusticola)* (14 in.) is reddish brown above, dark

below. It is found in woods, where its coloration camouflages it very well. It is largely nocturnal in habit. The display flight takes place at dusk and dawn, when the male will fly low over the trees calling with a soft, croaking voice. The flight itself is noiseless. One male will meet with several females, flying from one to the other during display. The bill is very well adapted for finding insects deep below the surface of the ground, as the tip is sensitive enough for the bird to recognise its prey (insect or worm) without seeing it. It is a highly prized game bird.

GREAT SNIPE

MAY-SEP

Woodcock

WOODCOCK

MAR-NOV

OCT-MAR

CURLEW (*Numenius arquata*) (22 in.) is a long-legged, brown Wader with a very long, down-curved bill. It nests on moors, meadows and marshes. On migration and in winter, it is seen on fields, meadows and on mud flats, often in flocks. The wing-beats are rather slow and deliberate. It often travels in groups in "V"-formations or lines. The name is an imitation of the plaintive whistle.

WHIMBREL (*Numenius phaeopus*) (16 in.) is quite similar to the Curlew, but has a shorter bill and a striped crown. It often associates with Curlews. The call is a short series of whistled notes. It is usually tamer than the Curlew. It nests on moorland and heath. The Whimbrel is rare in Europe in winter except in Southern Iberia.

BLACK-TAILED GODWIT (*Limosa limosa*) (16 in.) is a rather large, long-legged Wader with a long, straight bill. It has a solid black tip to the tail, in summer with chestnut coloured neck and breast. In winter these parts are grey. It nests in water meadows and marshes. It is often seen inland and is not as common along coasts as the Bar-tailed Godwit.

BAR-TAILED GODWIT (*Limosa lapponica*) (15 in.) is smaller and has shorter legs. The bill is slightly upturned. The tail is barred. In summer the body, head and neck are reddish brown, in winter, grey. Outside the breeding season, it is often found in quite large flocks along shores. Unlike the Black-tailed Godwit, it is only rarely met with on inland localities. Like the Black-tailed Godwit, it feeds by poking its bill into the mud.

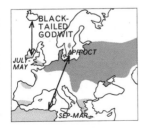

GREEN SANDPIPER (*Tringa ochropus*) (9 in.) is a rather small, dark above and white below with a conspicuous white rump. The underside of the wing is black. It breeds in woods with swamps and wet clearings, often using old nests of Thrushes. On migration and in winter, it is seen in swamps, marshes, ponds and streams. The call is a three-toned whistle, the first note mellow, the last two high-pitched in fast succession.

WOOD SANDPIPER (*Tringa glareola*) (8 in.) is very similar to the Green Sandpiper, but the upperside is not as dark and the contrast between the back and white rump not as pronounced. The underside of the wing is whitish. It nests in moors and bogs. Unlike the Green Sandpiper, it is rare in Europe during winter. It is not as wary as the Green Sandpiper. The flight call is an excited "chiff-chiff-chiff".

REDSHANK *(Tringa totanus)* (11 in.) is medium-sized, long-legged, grey, with a conspicuous white back and rump and a broad white band on the wing. The legs and bill are red. It is the most widespread and common of the larger Sandpipers. It nests in marshes, swamps and wet meadows. Outside the breeding season, it is usually seen on mud flats. The flight call is either a monosyllabic whistle or a trisyllabic whistle with the last two notes lower than the first.

SPOTTED REDSHANK *(Tringa erythropus)* (12 in.) is very similar to the Redshank in winter plumage, but lacks the white wing band. In summer it is black, speckled with white and has a white upper-rump extending far up on the back. On migration it is usually seen singly or in small parties, often associating with Redshanks and Greenshanks. The flight call is described as "chu-et".

GREATER YELLOWLEGS *(Tringa melanoleuca)* (14 in.) and **LESSER YELLOWLEGS** *(Tringa flavipes)* (10 in.) are vagrants from North America, mainly to the British Isles. Both are found on mud-flats and grassy marshes. The Greater Yellowlegs is not dissimilar to the Greenshank but is more spotted above. The legs are rich yellow, and the bill black with a green base. It is, on average, about one third larger than the Lesser Yellowlegs and has a longer, stouter bill which is slightly up-curved.

73

Greenshank

Common Sandpiper

GREENSHANK (*Tringa nebularia*) (12 in.) is grey, with white back and upper-rump, a long, slightly upturned bill and long green legs. It nests on moors and heath, outside the breeding season being found on mud flats and in flooded marshes, often associated with Redshanks and Spotted Redshanks. At a distance, the winter plumage looks quite whitish. The call is a loud, rather low-pitched whistle, usually repeated three times.

COMMON SANDPIPER (*Tringa hypoleucos*) (8 in.) is small and rather short-legged. It is dark greyish brown above, white below with a brown breast. The flight is characteristic. It flies low over the water, with the wing-tips pointing downwards and alternating periods of rapid wing-beats and gliding. It nests along streams and lakes and in winter is found on mud flats, and along shores of both fresh and salt water. It bobs its tail constantly. It is usually found singly or in small scattered groups.

GREENSHANK
APR-SEP
AUG-MAY

COMMON SANDPIPER
APR-SEP

KNOT *(Calidris canutus)* (10 in.) is chunky, rather short-billed and short-legged, red in summer with some dark marks above; grey above and white below in winter. The upper-rump is whitish. It breeds in the high Arctic and is, in winter, seen in flocks along seashores and on mud flats, often associating with the small Sandpipers.

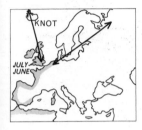

LITTLE STINT *(Calidris minuta)* (5 in.) is very small and short-legged, greyish brown above with white stripes, white below. The legs are black. On its travels, it is mainly seen on mud flats.

TEMMINCK'S STINT *(Calidris temminckii)* (5 in.) is very similar to the Little Stint. It has yellow legs, white on tail and no obvious markings on the back. It breeds in Northern Scandinavia, wintering from the Mediterranean coast south. It often associates with Little Stints and other "peeps".

winter

summer

winter

winter

winter

summer

summer

Dunlin

Curlew Sandpiper

DUNLIN (*Calidris alpina*) (7 in.) is in summer reddish-brown above, white below with a black patch on the belly. In winter it is brownish-grey above, white below with grey stripes on the breast. It is the most common of the small Sandpipers. It nests on moors and marshes. The nest is often situated under a tuft of grass, making it almost impossible to find. Outside the breeding season it is often seen in large flocks, sometimes numbering thousands of birds, on mud flats and shores. Single birds and smaller flocks are usually easy to approach, while larger flocks are quite wary. It feeds both by probing deep into the mud and picking snails and crustaceans on the surface. The song on the breeding grounds is a long, purring trill which is given both in flight and on the ground. The note given outside the breeding season is a short "tuup".

CURLEW SANDPIPER (*Calidris ferruginea*) (7 in.) is red, mottled with black above, in summer, and like the Dunlin in winter but with a white upper-rump and a slightly more curved bill. It is often seen in flocks with Dunlins, whose habits and habitats it shares. It breeds in Arctic Asia, migrating to the Southern hemisphere (South Africa and New Zealand) in early autumn. Along most coasts of Europe it is more common in autumn than in spring.

DUNLIN

JULY MAY

AUG MAY

76

Sanderling

Purple Sandpiper

summer

winter

PURPLE SANDPIPER (*Calidris maritima*) (8 in.) is very dark, only the belly being light in colour, and is a very robust looking bird with a short bill with a yellow base. It is usually seen in small flocks along rocky beaches. It does not often mix with other Sandpipers. It nests in northern

Broad-billed Sandpiper

Scandinavia and Iceland, in winter reaching the northern coast of France.

BROAD-BILLED SANDPIPER (*Limicola falcinellus*) (6½ in.) has, in summer, an almost Snipe-like pattern on the upper-side but in winter is more like the Dunlin, but has a clear white throat and eye stripe. The bill is flattened at the tip. The legs are shorter than those of the Dunlin. It

does not often associate with other Sandpipers. It nests in northern Scandinavia, migrating through eastern Europe to south-western Asia.

SANDERLING (*Calidris alba*) (8 in.) has a striking white wing-bar. In summer it is reddish-brown above and on head and breast, white below; in winter light grey above, white below with a black spot on the shoulder. The bill is straight and the legs are black. It is seen almost exclusively on sandy beaches, often in flocks, sometimes associating with other Sandpipers. It runs very fast, often following the waves up and down the beach, searching for small insects and snails. It is very active and almost resembles a running mouse. It is often very tame and easy to approach, as is frequently the case with birds breeding in the Arctic.

SANDERLING

JULY-JUNE

AUG-APR

Red-necked Phalarope

Ruff

RED-NECKED PHALAROPE *(Phalaropus lobatus)* (7 in.) in winter has colour pattern quite similar to that of the Dunlin. Unlike other Shorebirds, it is usually seen swimming and the toes are partially webbed and also lobed. In summer the female is more brightly coloured than the male and the male incubates the eggs and takes care of the young. It is usually quite maritime in its habits, in winter only being encountered inland accidently and usually only singly.

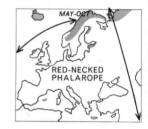

RUFF *(Philomachus pugmax)* (male 12 in., female 9 in.) is one of the most striking Waders in summer, when the male has a large ruff and two ear tufts. The colour of these ornaments varies. On the breeding grounds (meadows and marshes) certain sites are used for the display where the males fight with the females watching. The males are polygamous and it has been reported that one single male, the strongest, will mate with all females in the area. The female and the male in winter are dark brown above, whitish below with a sand coloured breast. The tail is blackish with white spots on the sides.

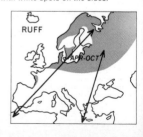

AVOCET *(Recurvirostra avosetta)*
(17 in.) is an extremely elegant,
long-legged Wader. The plumage
is white with black markings, the bill
long, thin and up-curved. In flight
the long, lead-coloured legs project
far beyond the short tail, making the
bird look like a thin cross. It feeds in
shallow water by skimming the surface
sideways with the bill, thus picking up
insects and micro-organisms. It nests
in colonies in marshes and meadows
close to shallow water.

BLACK-WINGED STILT
(Himantopus himantopus) (15 in.)
is white with a black back and wings,
extremely long, pink legs and a thin,
black, straight bill. It is unmistakable
both on ground and in flight where
the legs are stretched backwards.
It feeds by picking insects and snails
from the surface of shallow water.
It nests in colonies close to shallow
lagoons or flooded marshes. On land
it walks with long, deliberate strides.
The legs are so long (7 in.) it has to
bend them to reach the ground with
the bill. It is rare outside its regular
breeding and wintering area.

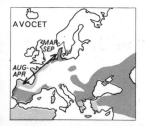

AVOCET

MAR-SEP

AUG-APR

BLACK-WINGED
STILT

APR-OCT

Stone Curlew

STONE
CURLEW

MAR-OCT

PRATINCOLE (*Glareola pratincola*) (10 in.) in flight looks very much like a giant swallow. It has a deeply forked tail and long, pointed wings. It will often catch insects in the air low over the ground or water. On ground the long wings and tail make it unmistakable. Its actions on ground are very similar to other Waders, and it runs well. It is quite gregarious and noisy. It is a summer visitor to Southern Spain, Southern France, Sicily, the Balkan countries and the Danube Basin.

STONE CURLEW (*Burhinus oedicnemus*) (16 in.) is a streaked brown and white bird. The bill is short and heavy, yellow at the base, black on the tip. The large yellow eye is characteristic, as are the two white wing stripes exposed in flight. It usually flies low over the ground with slow wing-beats, interrupted by gliding. When approached, it will often crouch, depending on its protective colouring for camouflage. It is found on dry and stony fields and heaths where its Curlew-like whistle is often heard, especially in the evening. It is often encountered in small groups. Unlike other Waders, it will lie down when resting. It lives on insects, worms and snails and will sometimes take frogs and mice.

Pratincole

GULLS AND TERNS

Gulls are medium-sized to large, long-winged and short-legged birds. Their plumage is mainly white when adult, the immatures being light brown and usually speckled. Most Gulls are seen along seashores, but some are also seen inland along lakes and rivers. They nest in colonies on seashores or along lakes. *Terns* are medium-sized to small, long-winged and short-legged birds. The tail is forked. They live on fish they catch by plunging head-first into the water. They nest in colonies. *Skuas* are brown birds, closely related to Gulls.

ARCTIC SKUA (*Stercorarius parasiticus*) (18 in.) occur in two colour phases. One is dark brown above, whitish below with a faint breast band. The other is dark brown all over. Adult birds have extended central tail feathers, which the dark-brown immatures lack. The wings are more pointed than those of the Gulls and the flight is more Hawk-like. Most of its life is spent at sea and it only comes on land for nesting. Although it feeds by itself, it obtains a large amount of its food by forcing other sea-birds to surrender their catch to it. It will pursue Gulls, Auks and Terns until they let their catch drop.

POMARINE SKUA (*Stercorarius pomarinus*) (20 in.) is very similar, but the elongated central feathers are very wide and it is considerably heavier and larger. It is rare. It nests

in the Arctic, spending the winter at sea.

GREAT SKUA (*Stercorarius skua*) (23 in.) is large and gull-like but is dark brown and has a much heavier build. The white mark near the end of the wing is visible in flight. It breeds in Iceland, the Faroes, Orkneys and Shetlands and is seen elsewhere in western Europe on migration.

APR-OCT

ARCTIC SKUA

Arctic Skua

im.

Great Black-backed Gull

Glaucous Gull

GREAT BLACK-BACKED GULL (*Larus marinus*) (29 in.) is the largest of the Gulls. The solid black back and wings are characteristic. The bill is very heavy, yellow with a red spot, the legs are flesh coloured. The adult plumage is not attained until about three years of age. The immatures go through various brown plumages but generally the plumage has more colour contrasts than that of the immatures of Herring Gulls and Lesser Black-backed Gulls. Like most Gulls, it lives from a great variety of food matter, such as molluscs, refuse, fish, etc., but this species is more of a Bird of Prey than others, especially in the summer season when it preys on chicks and eggs of other sea-birds.

GLAUCOUS GULL (*Larus hyperboreus*) (27 in.) has a very pale grey back and upper side of wing, without black markings on the wing-tips. The immature birds are in the first winter light buffish with white primaries. In the second winter the plumage is almost completely white. It is almost as big as the Great Black-backed Gull and the bill is as heavy. It resembles it closely in habits and they are both more marine in habit than the other large Gulls. It is not nearly as common as the Great Black-backed Gull.

GREAT BLACK-BACKED GULL

NOV-MAR

OCT-MAY

AUG-MAY

GLAUCOUS GULL

Lesser Black-backed Gull

im.

Herring Gull

LESSER BLACK-BACKED GULL (*Larus fuscus*) (21 in.) is, by some, considered a sub-species of the Herring Gull which it also resembles in habits and looks, except that the back and upper-side of wings is much darker, almost black. Pairs consisting of a Lesser Black-backed Gull and a Herring Gull can also be encountered. Unlike most other Gulls, it performs extensive migrations, reaching south to the Congo.

HERRING GULL (*Larus argentatus*) (22 in.) have grey back and wings with black and white wing-tips. The leg colours vary with the sub-species of which their are several in Europe, but are usually pink. They live on mussels, insects, worms, refuse etc. They will often follow fishing-boats and ferries to eat the refuse thrown overboard and will also congregate in large flocks on dumps and in harbours. The yellow bill has a red spot on the side. Biologists have found that this colour pattern is important when the young are being fed as they will peck at the red spot and this works as a stimulant for the parent bird to feed them. It is the most common of the large Gulls.

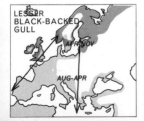

LESSER BLACK-BACKED GULL

APR-NOV

AUG-APR

HERRING GULL

Common Gull

Kittiwake

COMMON GULL (*Larus canus*) (16 in.) has a plumage similar to the Herring Gull, but has a small green bill and is much smaller. The immatures have a distinct black band on the end of the tail. Although its habits are very much like those of Herring Gull, it will more often be seen inland. following ploughs, and feeding on fields where it takes insects and worms. Although the nest is usually situated on the ground, it can rarely be found in low bushes.

KITTIWAKE (*Risa tridactyla*) (16 in.) is quite similar in plumage and size to the Common Gull, but has solid black wing-tips, black short legs and a yellow bill. The flight is more elegant. It is an oceanic bird, not often seen close to shore and practically never inland. It nests on steep cliffs in large colonies, placing the nest on very narrow ledges. The immatures have a dark "W" on the upper-side, a black band across the hind neck and a dark mark behind the eye. Immature birds also have a slightly forked tail.

COMMON GULL

AUG-APR

NOV-APR

KITTIWAKE

BLACK-HEADED GULL (*Larus ridibundus*) (15 in.) has grey wings with black and white wing-tips, red bill and legs and a characteristic dark brown hood in summer. In winter the hood is replaced by a single dark spot behind the eye. It is often seen inland and nests mainly along shallow bays and marshes and in wet moors. It often follows ploughs, picking up insects and worms. It is the most numerous European Gull.

LITTLE GULL (*Larus minutus*) (11 in.) is quite similar in having a hood. This hood, though, is solid black and extends further down on the hind neck. The under-wing of the adult bird is black. It has no black on the wing-tips. Although immature Black-headed Gulls have a brown "W" on the upper-side of the wings, this is not nearly as pronounced as on the Little Gull immatures. The flight is more Tern-like, and it often catches its food in flight. It is the smallest of the European Gulls.

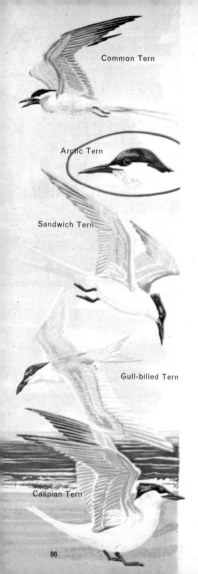

COMMON TERN (*Sterna hirundo*) (14 in.) is the most common of the European Terns. As most Terns, it is white with grey back and upperside of wings and a black cap extending from the bill to the hind neck. The bill is red with a black tip. It is usually seen fishing along shores, sometimes in flocks.

ARCTIC TERN (*Sterna paradisea*) (14 in.) has an all-red bill and the underside has a greyish tone. Otherwise it is very similar to the Common Tern. It nests along the Northern European coasts, south to Northern France. It migrates to Antarctic waters.

SANDWICH TERN (*Sterna sandvicensis*) (16 in.) is bigger and has a black bill with a yellow tip. The tail is comparatively short. It nests in large colonies, on the coast from Scandinavia to the Eastern Mediterranean, migrating to Africa in winter.

GULL-BILLED TERN (*Gelochelidon nilotica*) (15 in.) is quite similar to the Sandwich Tern, but has a shorter and more stout bill. It is a summer visitor to widely scattered breeding grounds in Denmark, Holland, along the Mediterranean and in the Danube Basin.

CASPIAN TERN (*Hydroprogne tschegrava*) (21 in.) is the largest of the Terns. The bill is very large and coral red. The wing tips are dark when seen from below. It is a summer visitor to the eastern part of the Baltic Sea and to the Black Sea, wintering in the eastern part of the Mediterranean and Africa.

COMMON TERN

APR-OCT

LITTLE TERN (*Sterna albifrons*) (10 in.) has a triangular white patch in front of the black cap. The bill is yellow with a black tip. It is the smallest of the Terns and is mainly seen along sandy beaches where it nests in small colonies.

Little Tern

BLACK TERN (*Chlidonias niger*) (10 in.) is blackish in summer with white under-tail coverts. In winter it is dark grey above, with a cap, white below. It nests along inland lakes and marshes and fishes from fresh water. In winter it is also seen along coasts with other Terns. The wings are broader than other Terns and the flight more fluttering.

WHISKERED TERN (*Chlidonias hybrida*) (10 in.) is quite similar to the Black Tern, but has white cheeks and a red bill. It resembles the Black Tern in its behaviour and habitat. It is a summer visitor to the Iberian Peninsula, southern France, the Danube Basin and southern Russia.

Black Tern

Whiskered Tern

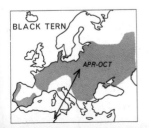

AUKS *(Sub-order Alcae)* belong to the same order as the Waders, Gulls and Terns. They are medium-sized black and white diving birds. They only come on land to breed. They nest in colonies on rocky sea-cliffs. The flight is straight and fairly fast, with extremely rapid wing-beats.

Guillemot

summer

winter

Razorbill

winter

summ

GUILLEMOT *(Uria aalge)* (17 in.) is dark brown above, white below, with a dark brown breast in summer; in winter it has a white breast and throat and a conspicuous black streak extending back from the eye. The bill is long, rather narrow and pointed. It does not build a nest, but lays its single egg, which is very long and pear-shaped, on a ledge. The colonies often consist of enormous numbers of birds.

RAZORBILL *(Alca torda)* (16 in.) is blacker than the Guillemot and has a heavier bill with a white line through it. In winter it has a white throat. Like the Guillemot, it lays its egg on ledges. It also stands upright when perched. On the water it looks more compact and plump. Unlike the Guillemot it will often nest on rocky shores without cliffs.

GUILLEMOT

RAZORBILL

AUG-MAY

Black Guillemot

winter

summer

winter

summer

Puffin

juv.

BLACK GUILLEMOT (*Cepphus grylle*) (13 in.) in summer is all black with a white patch on the wing. In winter it is light grey with a darker upper-side. It nests in holes or under cliffs, not in colonies with other Auks. It is, in general, not as sociable as the other Auks. When perched, the body is held almost horizontal.

PUFFIN (*Fratercula arctica*) (12 in.) in summer has a huge red, blue and yellow bill and grey cheeks. In winter

the bill is smaller and dull in colour. It nests in holes dug into grassy slopes.

LITTLE AUK (*Plautus alle*) (8 in.) is by far the smallest of the Auks. In summer it has black upper-side, throat and breast, and white belly; in winter, black upper-side but white throat and breast. It breeds in huge colonies in the Arctic, in winter reaching south to the North Sea and northern part of the Atlantic.

BLACK GUILLEMOT

PUFFIN

OCT-APR

SANDGROUSE *(Pteroclidae)* are pigeon-like light brown birds with pointed wings and tail. They are usually seen on the ground, where they feed in flocks. They are resident in Spain, Portugal and southern-most France.

DOVES AND PIGEONS *(Columbidae)* are medium-sized plump birds with small heads and pointed wings. Outside the breeding season they are often seen in large flocks.

Rock Dove

Pin-tailed Sandgrouse

ROCK DOVE

ROCK DOVE *(Columba livia)* (13 in.) is the ancestor of the domestic Pigeon. It is greyish blue with a white upper rump and two narrow black wing stripes. Its cooing is well known. Unlike other Doves it rarely settles in trees. It nests in crevices in rocky cliffs, particularly along coasts. The domestic form has taken advantage of the artificial cliffs and nesting sites furnished by large stone buildings. It often travels in small flocks. The flight is fast. It lives on grain and other seeds. Like most doves it usually lays only two eggs and the nest is very flimsily built, consisting of only a few twigs.

Stock Dove

Wood Pigeon

WOOD PIGEON *(Columba palumbus)* (16 in.) is the largest European Pigeon. It is distinguished by its two white spots on the sides of the neck, and in flight by a white stripe on the upper side of the wing. Outside the breeding season it is often seen in large flocks on fields close to woods. It nests in trees in parks, hedgerows and woods. When it is flushed from a tree it flies off with a loud clatter of the wings.

STOCK DOVE *(Columba oenas)* (13 in.) is very similar to the Rock Dove but lacks the white upper rump and the black stripes on the wing are less distinct. It nests in holes in trees. It is often seen with Wood

Pigeons, but in much smaller numbers. The flight is faster than that of the Wood Pigeon and the wing-beats more rapid.

WOOD PIGEON

MAR-OCT

Turtle Dove

Collared Turtle Dove

TURTLE DOVE (*Streptopelia turtur*) (11 in.) is reddish, darker above, lighter below, with a blue and white striped mark on each side of the neck. The rather long tail is black, bordered with white. It is found in open woods, fields with many bushes, parks and similar habitats, often in small groups. It feeds on cultivated fields. The wing-beats are more jerky than other doves.

COLLARED TURTLE DOVE (*Streptopelia decaocto*) (11 in.) is yellow-brown with a narrow black band across the hind neck. The tail is white with only a small black area at the base. It nests on buildings and on ledges in towns and villages. In recent years it has spread to the north-west from its original range in south-eastern Europe. It feeds on the ground. The nest is built in trees and it has a preference for conifers. The voice is a very characteristic "coo-cooo-cuk".

TURTLE DOVE

APR-OCT

COLLARED TURTLE DOVE

CUCKOOS (Cuculiformes) are long tailed and rather long winged medium-sized birds. Their feet are exceptional as they have two toes pointed forwards and two backwards. The two species found in Europe are both parasitic in that they lay their eggs in the nests of other birds.

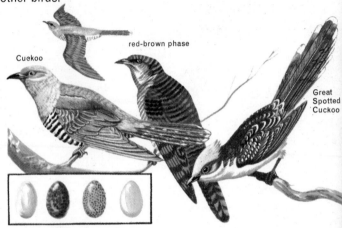

red-brown phase

Cuckoo

Great Spotted Cuckoo

CUCKOO (*Cuculus canorus*) (13 in.) is grey except for the belly, which is white, barred with black. Some females are red-brown and barred. The call of the Cuckoo is unmistakable and known to every child. In spring

CUCKOO

APR-SEP

the female lays its eggs in the nests of song-birds, only one egg in each nest. The egg generally corresponds in size and colour to that of the hosts. The young develop more quickly in the egg than the young of the host, and immediately after being hatched the Cuckoo young will work its way under the other eggs and throw them out of the nest. The foster-parents will then feed it. Cuckoos live on caterpillars and other insects.

GREAT SPOTTED CUCKOO (*Clamator glandarius*) (15 in.) is black and white with a very long tail. It lays its eggs in the nests of Magpies and other large corvidae, often several eggs in the same nest. It is a summer visitor to Spain and Portugal.

grey-phase

reddish-brown phase

Tawny Owl

Ural Owl

OWLS *(Strigiformes)* are large to medium-sized Birds of Prey with large heads. The eyes are big and facing forward, surrounded by a "disc" of short feathers. The beak is short and hooked, the feet covered with feathers. They are mainly nocturnal. The flight is noiseless.

TAWNY OWL *(Strix aluco)* (15 in.) is the most common of the Owls. Two types occur with different colour faces, a grey and a reddish brown. It nests in holes in trees or in the old nests of other birds. The 2—4 eggs are white. It is common in gardens, parks and woods. The hooting is often heard at night. It also has a shrill "ee-ick" call. It mainly lives on mice caught at night. Sometimes it will strike people approaching the nesting site.

URAL OWL *(Strix uralensis)* (24 in.) looks quite similar to Tawny Owl, but has smaller eyes, more striped plumage, longer tail and is larger. It is found in large woods where it breeds in hollow trees.

TAWNY OWL

URAL OWL

Barn Owl

juv.

Tengmalm's Owl

BARN OWL (*Tyto alba*) (14 in.) is yellow brown above, white below. The "discs" around the eyes form a characteristic heart-shaped figure. The legs are comparatively long. The population in north and eastern Europe has a darker back and the underside is reddish, not white. It nests in buildings, hollow trees and crevices in rocks. The call is a wild shriek. It hunts mice at night, locating them by its excellent hearing.

TENGMALM'S OWL (*Aegolius funereus*) (10 in.) has a very large head and comparatively long tail. The large spots on the plumage are characteristic, as is the upright posture when perched. It lives in coniferous forests, usually in mountain areas. The call, which is often heard, is a rapid succession, about five "eoo"-like whistles.

BARN OWL

TENGMALM'S OWL

Scops Owl

SCOPS OWL *(Otus scops)* (8 in.) is a very small brown Owl with rather inconspicuous ear-tufts. It has a very slim build. It lives on insects. The call is a repeated sad whistle. It is found in open woods, parks, gardens and along roads.

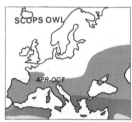

LITTLE OWL *(Athene noctua)* (9 in.) has a flat head and a plump form. It is often seen during daytime in open country with scattered trees. The flight is characteristic, undulating like that of the woodpeckers. It is resident all over Europe, north to Scotland, Sweden and Finland.

PYGMY OWL *(Glaucidium passerinum)* (7 in.) is the smallest of the European Owls. It lives in forests of mountainous regions. It is often seen during the day. Various whistling calls are often heard.

Little Owl

Pygmy Owl

LONG-EARED OWL *(Asio otus)* (14 in.) is mottled brown with two long feathered tufts over the eyes—"horns". It nests particularly in coniferous forests, using old nests of other birds for breeding. It is found all over Europe, north to northern Scandinavia, only withdrawing from the northern-most part of the breeding range during winter.

SHORT-EARED OWL *(Asio flammeus)* (15 in.) is dark brown above, light brown with stripes below, and has two short horns. It is found in open country—fields and marshes, where it nests on the ground. It often hunts during the day. In flight the wing-tips are held upwards, forming a "V".

EAGLE OWL *(Bubo bubo)* (27 in.) looks like a giant Long-eared Owl. It is found in woods, usually in rocky country. The call is a very deep, far-reaching "boo-hu". Like the Long-eared Owl it is nocturnal.

Long-eared Owl

Short-eared Owl

Eagle Owl

Nightjar

NIGHTJARS *(Caprimulgiformes)* are medium-sized, long-tailed and long-winged nocturnal birds. The feet are small and weak, the bill small but the mouth wide. One American kind of Nightjar is the only bird that has been proved to hibernate.

NIGHTJAR *(Caprimulgus europaeus)* (11 in.) is very dark brown, the male with white spots near the wing-tips and white tip of tail. The head is broad and flat and the eyes rather large. During the day it usually sits

NIGHTJAR

APR-OCT

motionless perched lengthways along a branch or on the ground, its colours matching that of the background. At night it catches moths and other insects in the air. The flight is elegant and silent with sudden twists and turns. The wing-beats are deliberate. The song is a sustained rapid churring, usually only heard at night. The two white eggs are laid on the ground on heathland or in open woodland.

RED-NECKED NIGHTJAR *(Caprimulgus ruficollis)* (12 in.) is very similar to the Nightjar, but a little bigger and has a white throat. The song is a repeated double note. It is found as a summer visitor to the dry areas of southern Spain and Portugal.

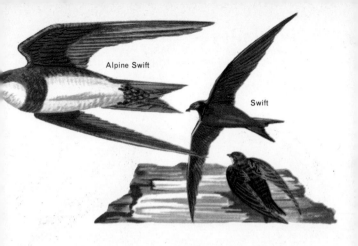

Alpine Swift

Swift

SWIFTS *(Apodiformes)* are small birds with long narrow wings and a big mouth with which they catch insects in the air. They are known to be able to sleep while flying. The feet are very small and they are not able to take flight from flat ground. The edible Swallow nests are really the nests of Swifts, breeding in China.

SWIFT *(Apus apus)* (7 in.) is dark brown, except for a white throat. It breeds under roofs or in rocky cliffs. It is often seen in large flocks, especially at dusk and dawn. The flight is very characteristic, the scythe-like wings beating rapidly interrupted by long glides. The voice is harsh and screaming.

ALPINE SWIFT *(Alpus melba)* (8 in.) is light brown above, white below with a brown breast band. It is found in rocky country where it nests in colonies. It is known to be one of the fastest fliers among the birds. It closely resembles the Swift in behaviour.

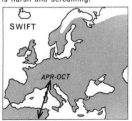

SWIFT

APR-OCT

ALPINE SWIFT

APR-OCT

KINGFISHERS AND THEIR ALLIES

(Coraciiformes) form a rather heterogenous order of colourful birds. Most are tropical and only four species of four different families are found in Europe. All of these nest in holes.

Kingfisher

Bee-eater

KINGFISHER (*Alcedo atthis*) (7 in.) is a small bird with large head and bill. It is brilliant blue-green above, reddish brown below—it has been described as the "flying diamond". It is found along rivers, streams and lakes where it nests in a hole dug out in small cliffs. It lives on fish caught by plunging into the water head-first from a perch, where it will sit patiently waiting for the opportunity. It flies low over the water with rapid wing-beats. The call is a repeated shrill shriek.

BEE-EATER (*Merops apiaster*) (11 in.) is very colourful, has pointed wings and elongated tail feathers. When perched it sits in a rather upright position with its long pointed bill angled slightly upwards. The flight is elegant and swallow-like. It is almost always seen in flocks and also nests colonially in holes in banks and clay cliffs. Its food consists of insects which are caught in the air.

KINGFISHER

BEE-EATER

APR-OCT

Roller

Hoopoe

ROLLER (*Coracias garrulus*) (12 in.) is light blue with a reddish-brown back. The build of the bird suggests a Jay and, although the flight silhouette is quite similar to the flight silhouette of Jays and other corvine birds, the wing action is much more rapid and resembles that of the Pigeon. Although it is sometimes seen on the ground, where it hops clumsily, it is most often perched on a branch or other exposed site on the look-out for insects, which it usually takes from the ground. It nests in holes in trees.

HOOPOE (*Upupa epops*) (11 in.) is light brown with a large fan-shaped crest which it can erect at will and, most strikingly, a bold pattern of black and white on upper-side of wings, back and tail. The wings are very rounded and the flight almost butterfly-like. The bill is long and slightly curved. It is most often seen on the ground, feeding on insects and larvae. Although it nests in holes in trees, cliffs or walls, it is most often seen in open country. The name is an imitation of its call.

ROLLER

APR-SEP

HOOPOE

APR-OCT

WOODPECKERS are short-tailed, broad-winged birds with undulating flight. The bill is chisel-shaped for boring tree trunks. They also nest in holes bored out in trees. Of the four toes, two point backward, two forward. They all have very long tongues to which insects and larvae stick.

Green Woodpecker

Grey-headed Woodpecker

Black Woodpecker

GREEN WOODPECKER (*Picus viridis*) (13 in.) has a green back and red cap. It is resident in deciduous forests and parks all over Europe, except Ireland and northern-most Scandinavia. To a large degree it lives on ants it digs out of ant-nests in the ground. Unlike most other Woodpeckers, it is only rarely heard drumming.

GREY-HEADED WOODPECKER (*Picus canus*) (10 in.) is very similar, but only has a small red spot over the bill and is more grey underneath. The female lacks the red front. It is a resident of deciduous woods of Eastern and Central Europe and the middle part of the Scandinavian Peninsula.

BLACK WOODPECKER (*Dryocopus martius*) (18 in.) is all black except for a red cap. It is the biggest of the European Woodpeckers. It breeds in coniferous and beech woods.

BLACK WOODPECKER

SPOTTED WOODPECKERS have black backs and wings with white patterns, white breast and belly, usually some red on the under-tail coverts and a pattern of white and black on the head. Males also have red on crown. They occur in woods, parks and gardens.

Great Spotted Woodpecker

GREAT SPOTTED WOOD-PECKER (Dendrocopus major) (9 in.) male has a small red spot on the hind neck. The immature has a red cap. This, plus two large white patches on the back, is characteristic.

LESSER SPOTTED WOOD-PECKER (Dendrocopus minor) (6 in.) male has a red cap and the back is barred with white. Immatures and females are similar, but lack the red cap.

MIDDLE SPOTTED WOOD-PECKER (Dendrocopus medius) (8 in.) has white spots on the back like the Great and a red cap like the Lesser. It is a resident locally on the Continent, north as far as Southern Sweden.

Lesser Spotted Woodpecker

Middle Spotted Woodpecker

Three-toed Woodpecker

White-backed Woodpecker

WRYNECK *(Jynx torquilla)* (7 in.) is brown above with darker and lighter spots, lighter below with dark brown bars. The bill is very short and stout. It is closely related to the Woodpeckers, although it looks quite different. Its name is derived from the habit of turning the head through 180 degrees. Like Woodpeckers, it nests in holes in trees, but it is not able to excavate these itself. It feeds on insects on the ground. It is rather wary and secretive in habits and more often heard than seen. The voice is a mi-auing, repeated "cue".

WHITE-BACKED WOODPECKER *(Dendrocopus leucotos)* (10 in.) is the largest of the Spotted Woodpeckers. It has a white upper-rump and the underside is striped. The male has a red cap. It is a resident in the hilly woods of Eastern and Central Europe, Central Scandinavia and locally in the Pyrenees.

THREE-TOED WOODPECKER *(Picoides tridactylus)* (9 in.) is almost completely black on the head, hind neck and upper-side except for a broad white stripe reaching from the hind neck down. The sides are barred. The male has a small yellow crown. As the name indicates, it only has three toes. It is found mainly in coniferous woods.

Wryneck

THREE-TOED WOODPECKER

WRYNECK

MAR-SEP

SEP-APR

egg of Blackbird

7 days

1 day

Blackbird

20 days

Goldcrest

Raven

egg of Raven

PERCHING BIRDS *(Passeriformes)* These constitute the most important order of birds and represent over half of the existing species. All the European species are placed in the sub-order of Songbirds *(Passeres)* and many of their beautiful songs are sufficiently characteristic to identify them. The order includes an extremely diverse collection of species. Their sizes range from the Raven to the tiny Goldcrest; in the form of the bill from the large and strong beak of the Pine Gosbeak to the tiny bill of the Swallow, and their habitats from the luxurious tree tops where the Wood Warbler is found to the mountain torrents which form the home of the Dipper.

In contrast to this wide variation the common features of the order may seem almost negligible but they are no less important. The perching feet, with four unwebbed toes, three forward, one behind, are perfectly adapted for seizing the small branches on which these birds alight. After hatching the naked young remain in the nest for a long period and are fed by their parents. Although the identification of Passerines seems complicated to the newcomer to ornithology, careful observation will soon enable him to recognize a large number of species.

LARKS (Alaudidae) are small to medium-sized brown birds, nesting on the ground. The claw of the hind toe is elongated. The sexes are similar. The song is musical and is often given while the bird is in flight, but also on the ground. Outside the breeding season Larks are often seen in loose flocks.

Skylark

Short-toed Lark

SKYLARK (Alauda arvensis) (7 in.) has a streaked breast and white outer tail feathers, but otherwise no distinct markings. It sometimes shows a trace of a crest, but never as obvious as that of the Crested Lark. It is found in open fields and meadows, singing its familiar flight song. It is one of the most numerous of European birds and one of the few birds for which the spreading of agriculture in Europe has been an advantage.

SHORT-TOED LARK (Calandrella cinerea) (6 in.) is much smaller. It is streaked above, but the underside is light and unstriped. On both sides of the neck it has a rather indistinct dark spot. The bill is short. The flight is characteristically undulating and usually low over the ground. It is usually found in dryer situations than the Skylark

SKYLARK

FEB-NOV

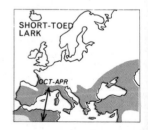

SHORT-TOED LARK

OCT-APR

CALANDRA LARK (*Melanocorypha calandra*) (8 in.) has a thick bill and a black patch on each side of the neck. It is resident along the Mediterranean, where it is found mainly on dry fields.

WOOD LARK (*Lullula arborea*) (6 in.) looks very much like a very short-tailed Skylark. It nests in open woods, open land with bushes and heath. The song is melodious with characteristic trills.

CRESTED LARK (*Galerida cristata*) (7 in.) has a long crest and triangular reddish brown patches on the tail. It is usually seen in dry areas, often near roads and towns. It is a resident of Continental Europe, north to Southern Sweden and Finland.

THEKLA LARK (*Galerida theklae*) (6 in.) is almost identical to the Crested Lark, but has more clearly marked stripes on the breast and a slightly shorter bill. It is a resident of the Iberian Peninsula.

SHORE LARK (*Eremophila alpestris*) (7 in.) has a characteristic facial pattern with two short horns. It breeds in Northern Scandinavia and is, in winter, found along North Sea coasts, usually on marshes and sandbanks.

Calandra Lark

Wood Lark

Crested Lark

Shore Lark

WOOD LARK

MAR-NOV

SWALLOWS AND MARTINS are small, long-winged birds with graceful flight. The feet are small and only used for sitting, not walking. They live from insects caught in the air. In the autumn they gather in large flocks for migration.

Swallow

House Martin

SWALLOW (*Hirundo rustica*) (8 in.) is metallic blue-black above, white to rusty below, with a black breast and red throat. The tail is very long and deeply forked. It builds its open nest from mud in barns and on other buildings. It has a pleasant twittering song, often given from a perch on wires.

RED-RUMPED SWALLOW (*Hirundo daurica*) (7 in.) is quite similar, but has white throat and rusty upper-rump. It is a summer visitor

HOUSE MARTIN

APR-OCT

to Southern Spain and the southern part of the Balkan Peninsula.

SWALLOW

APR-OCT

HOUSE MARTIN (*Delichon urbica*) (5 in.) is black above, except for pure white upper-rump, white below with a forked tail. It builds its closed nest from mud on buildings, often in towns. In spring they can be seen collecting building material in muddy puddles. It nests in colonies. Its flight is not as agile as that of the Swallow, the wing-beats being faster and stiffer. Like other Swallows, it drinks by dipping its bill in the water while flying.

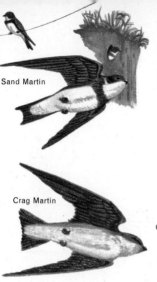

Sand Martin

Crag Martin

CRAG MARTIN (*Hirundo rupestris*) (6 in.) is brown above, dirty white below with a square tail. It builds oval clay nests on rocky cliffs, often in colonies. It is found in the Mediterranean region, in winter only withdrawing from the northern-most part of its range.

Golden Oriole

ORIOLES

GOLDEN ORIOLE (*Oriolus oriolus*) (10 in.) belongs to a family of its own. It is a Thrush-like yellow bird with black wings and tail. Females and immatures are greenish, streaked below, with dark rings on the tail. It is usually seen in mature deciduous forests and parks, moving around high in the foliage in its search for insects. The flight is undulating. The nest is a woven cup hanging underneath a fork in a high branch. The full, melodious, far-ranging whistle has been described as "weela-weelo".

SAND MARTIN (*Riparia riparia*) (5 in.) is brown above, white below with a brown breast band and a slightly forked tail. It nests in colonies in holes bored in banks or cliffs. The colonies are often very large.

SAND MARTIN

APR-OCT

GOLDEN ORIOLE

APR-AUG

CROWS (Corvidae) are large, perching birds. Their bills are rather long, straight and powerful. The feet and legs are rather weak. The wings are rounded. The sexes are similar. Most build rather large bulky nests in trees. The eggs are greenish with spots.

Raven

RAVEN

RAVEN *(Corvus corax)* (25 in.) is the largest kind of Crow. It is black with a very large, strong bill. The tail is long and slightly pointed. It is often seen soaring, like Buzzards and Eagles. It lives mainly on carrion, but will also take smaller animals, a habit which has given it a bad reputation and caused a severe decline in the population. It is now mainly found in mountains where it builds its nest on ledges, but it will also build the nest in trees. The call is a very characteristic deep, harsh "koaarp".

Hooded Crow

Carrion Crow

HOODED CROW (*Corvus cornix*) (19 in.) is grey with black head, wings and tail. The tail is square. The bill is thick. Outside the breeding season it is often seen in flocks. The food consists mainly of insects, carrion and garbage. It nests in trees, often very high up, but will feed on open fields.

CARRION CROW (*Corvus corone*) (19 in.) is all black. It can be told from the Raven by the smaller size and square tail and from immature Rooks by the shape of head and bill (see drawing on p. 112). It is similar to the Hooded Crow in habitat and behaviour and is even considered, by some, to be a sub-species of it. In areas where both species of Crow nest, mixed pairs consisting of one Hooded Crow and one Carrion Crow are quite common and hybirds are numerous. These hybirds show various amounts of grey in the same pattern as the Hooded Crow.

HOODED CROW
MAR-NOV
OCT-APR

CARRION CROW

Carrion Crow   Immature Rook

Rook

Jackdaw

Magpie

ROOK *(Corvus frugilegus)* (18 in.) is metallic black. The immediate surroundings of the bill of the adult bird are naked, which can be seen from far away as a light grey patch, while the immatures have completely black heads like the Carrion Crow. The shape of the bill, though, is a good field mark and is slimmer and straighter than that of the Carrion Crow. It nests in colonies in tall trees, usually at the edge of a wood, in a park or in small clumps of trees close to open fields. It is usually seen in flocks. The food consists of insects and seeds.

JACKDAW *(Corvus monedula)* (13 in.) is black with grey hind neck and sides of face. It walks with a characteristic nodding of the head. It is very sociable and is usually seen in flocks, sometimes with other birds like Starlings and Rooks. It nests in hollow trees, chimneys and old nests of other birds. Rookeries sometimes contain a few pairs of Jackdaws. The call is a characteristic "tjack". It is found both summer and winter all over Europe, except northern-most Scandinavia and Iceland.

MAGPIE *(Pica pica)* (18 in.) is metallic black with a white belly and a large white patch on the wings. The long tail makes it unmistakable. It builds its large domed nest in scattered trees in farmland and parks. It is attracted by shiny objects and in the nest one will often find odds and ends made of metal. It lives from insects, carrion and seeds etc. It is usually seen singly or in pairs, although larger gatherings can be met with. The flight is laborious and ungraceful. It is a resident all over Europe, except for a few Mediterranean islands and Iceland.

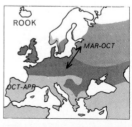

ROOK

MAR-OCT

OCT-APR

JAY *(Garrulus glandarius)* (14 in.) is a colourful bird of woods and parks. Although usually seen singly, in some winters it will gather in flocks. It lives from acorns and other fruits, occasionally insects, and will sometimes take eggs. It is a resident, found all over Europe, except northernmost Scandinavia, Scotland and Iceland.

NUTCRACKER *(Nucifraga caryocatactes)* (13 in.) is brown with white spots, a short black tail and white under-tail coverts. It is found in summer in coniferous forests, in winter in mixed woods and gardens. Outside the breeding season it is quite sociable and is usually met with in small flocks. In autumn Nutcrackers collect large numbers of nuts, hiding them. In winter, when food is scarce, they return to these stores.

CHOUGH *(Pyrrhocorax pyrrhocorax)* (16 in.) is glossy black with a long curved red bill and red legs. It is a bird of mountainous landscapes, sometimes found on sea-cliffs. It is a resident of the western coast of Great Britain and Ireland, Normandy, the Mediterranean area and the Alps.

ALPINE CHOUGH *(Pyrrhocorax graculus)* (15 in.) is similar to the Chough, but with a shorter yellow bill. It is a resident of the mountainous areas of Mediterranean countries.

Jay

Nutcracker

Chough

Alpine Chough

NUTCRACKER

TITS (*Paridae*) are small, lively birds with short bills. Many nest in holes in trees and they are easily attracted by nest-boxes. They live mainly on insects they catch in trees among the foliage, but will also take fat and meat. Outside the breeding season they are often seen in mixed flocks. Tits are generally single brooded and this is unusual for a small bird.

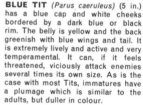

GREAT TIT (*Parus major*) (6 in.) has a black head and breast, white cheeks, a yellow belly with a black line down the centre, and greenish back. It is the largest of the Tits and is found in almost every garden and wood. In spring its characteristic and familiar "teacher" is repeated over and over again.

BLUE TIT (*Parus caeruleus*) (5 in.) has a blue cap and white cheeks bordered by a dark blue or black rim. The belly is yellow and the back greenish with blue wings and tail. It is extremely lively and active and very temperamental. It can, if it feels threatened, viciously attack enemies several times its own size. As is the case with most Tits, immatures have a plumage which is similar to the adults, but duller in colour.

GREAT TIT

BLUE TIT

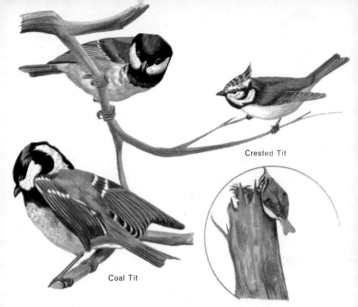

Crested Tit

Coal Tit

COAL TIT *(Parus ater)* (4 in.) has a black head and white cheeks and a large white spot on the hind neck. The underside is buffish white, the back, tail and wings grey. It is found mainly in coniferous woods, where its plaintive whistle is often heard. When climbing in the branches on the look-out for insects, it will often hang upside down, as is the habit of many other Tits.

CRESTED TIT *(Parus cristatus)* (5 in.) has a greyish brown upperside, buffish white under-side, white cheeks with a narrow, black border, and a big, barred crest. It is almost exclusively found in coniferous woods, where it nests in holes in tree-stumps. It has a very characteristic low-pitched purring note. Besides finding insects in the branches, it is sometimes seen sitting on tree trunks finding its food in the cracks of the bark.

COAL TIT

CRESTED TIT

Marsh Tit

Willow Tit

Sombre Tit

Long-tailed Tit

northern form

MARSH TIT *(Parus palustris)* (5 in.) is greyish brown, lighter below, darker above, with a black cap and chin. It is found in deciduous woods, thickets and gardens with many bushes and trees.

MARSH TIT

WILLOW TIT *(Parus atricapillus)* (5 in.) is almost identical to the Marsh Tit, but has duller black cap, slightly more black on chin and white patch on wing. It is found in swampy woods, particularly amongst willows.

SOMBRE TIT *(Parus lugubris)* (6 in.) has a similar colour pattern but much heavier build. It is a resident of the Balkan countries.

LONG-TAILED TIT *(Aegithalos caudatus)* (6 in.) is black and white with a very long tail. The nest is domed and found in thickets. It is a resident all over Europe, except northern-most Scandinavia and Iceland. It is found mainly in gardens and thickets.

WILLOW TIT

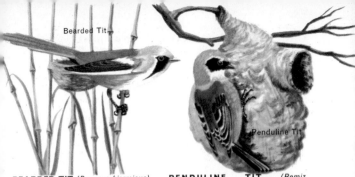
Bearded Tit

Penduline Tit

BEARDED TIT *(Panurus biarmicus)* (7 in.) is tawny above with a white breast. The male has a grey head with a conspicuous black moustache. The female has a dull coloured brown head. It is found almost exclusively in large reed beds.

PENDULINE TIT *(Remiz pendulinus)* (4 in.) is the smallest of the European Tits. It has a conspicuous black mask and a chestnut back. It is found usually in marshy areas, where it builds a domed nest with a funnel-shaped entrance, in thickets or bushes.

BEARDED TIT

PENDULINE TIT

NUTHATCHES *(Sittidae)* are small Woodpecker-like, perching birds. Unlike Woodpeckers, they are capable of running down tree trunks. The sexes are similar. They nest in holes. Three species are found in Europe, of which only one is common and widespread.

NUTHATCH *(Sitta europaea)* (6 in.) is blue above, white with various amounts of red underneath, and has a distinct black stripe through the eye. The bill is pointed and strong. It is most often found in mature, deciduous woods. It climbs a tree in its search for insects. It will also eat seeds and is easily attracted to bird tables. It nests in cavities in trees, filling up the entrance hole with mud until it has attained a suitable size.

Nuthatch

CREEPERS (Certhiidae) are small birds with long, thin and curved bills. The feet are weak, the tail rather short. The sexes are similar.

Tree Creeper

woodland. In southern Europe the Short-toed Tree Creeper can be found at all altitudes up to about 5,000 ft., while the Tree Creeper here is only found in the highlands.

WALL CREEPER (*Tichodroma muraria*) (7 in.) is black, grey and white with large red patches on the wings. The flight is very fluttering, almost butterfly-like. It is often seen climbing on rocks looking for insects in the crevices. It is usually found in mountains above a height of 6,000 ft. in summer and at lower altitudes in winter.

Wall Creeper

summer

winter

TREE CREEPER (*Certhia familiaris*) (5 in.) is striped brown above, white below. It climbs up tree trunks looking for insects. It nests in cracks in the bark of trees in woods and parks.

SHORT-TOED TREE CREEPER (*Certhia brachydactyla*) (5 in.) is similar, but has brown flanks and a longer bill and its song lacks the high-pitched notes characteristic of the Tree Creeper. It is resident in Continental Europe south of Scandinavia. Both species are usually found in parks, gardens and open

TREE CREEPER

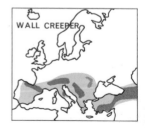

WALL CREEPER

DIPPERS AND WRENS *(Cinclidae and Troglodytidae)*

are closely related and, although usually quite different in size, they all share the same general build, which is a rather stocky body, short neck and very short tail which is often held cocked. The bills are pointed. These birds are very lively.

DIPPER *(Cinclus cinclus)* (7 in.) is dark brown with a clear white throat and breast. It has a characteristic habit of always bobbing up and down when standing. It nests along fast-flowing streams, usually in mountains. In winter it prefers the same locations, but will sometimes be seen along lakes and seashores. It often perches on stones in the middle of streams. It lives on insects it catches under water, and it is able to run on the river bottom.

It swims well, either on or under water. The flight is straight and low over the water.

WREN *(Troglodytes troglodytes)* (4 in.) is brown. It is darker above, lighter below, and the flanks, wings and short tail are barred. It usually feeds on insects close to the ground in thick vegetation. It is very active, always scooting around. It builds a globular nest in holes or in thickets. The alarm note is a repeated metallic click, and the song a very loud melodious warbling given from a low perch. Unlike most birds, it sings almost all the year round.

Dipper

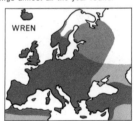
WREN

DIPPER
OCT–APR

Wren

THRUSHES (_Turdinae_) are medium-sized, long-tailed, long-legged perching birds with pointed bill and wings. They are all good singers. Besides the Thrushes, the family also contains Warbler-like birds like the Redstart and the Nightingale. These are grouped with the Thrushes because of minute anatomical similarities.

MISTLE THRUSH (_Turdus viscivorus_) (11 in.) is brown above, white with heavy dark brown spots below. It is similar in colour pattern to the Song Thrush, but much bigger. It is found in mature, open woods, in parks and along edges of forests. The song is very musical, but the call is a characteristic rasping chatter. Outside the breeding season it is not uncommon to find it in fields and other open areas, although it has a preference for openings bordered by trees or bushes.

FIELDFARE (_Turdus pilaris_) (10 in.) has a bluish grey head and rump, a chestnut back and a spotted breast. It breeds along wood margins, usually in colonies. In winter it is usually seen in open fields in flocks, which are sometimes of great size. There can be a great variation in size between the different individuals. The call is a nasal "tchek", often repeated several times.

Mistle Thrush

Fieldfare

Redwing

Song Thrush

SONG THRUSH (*Turdus philomelos*) (9 in.) is common in almost every garden, park and wood. It is uniformly brown above, spotted below. It is somewhat similar to the Mistle Thrush, but it is much smaller. The nest is placed in bushes or trees and the nest cup is lined with clay, making it very solid. The eggs are greenish blue lightly spotted with black. It mainly lives on snails, worms, insects and berries. The song is melodious, usually given from a high perch.

REDWING (*Turdus iliacus*) (8 in.) is brown above, striped below, and has chestnut coloured flanks. It is quite similar to the Song Thrush in size and shape, but has a conspicuous, white superciliary stripe. It breeds in woodlands, in particular those with birch, and is in winter most often seen on open fields and grassland or in open woods. At this time of year it often mixes with Fieldfares. Like the Song Thrush, it often migrates at night and one can hear its soft call note, especially on dark nights in the migratory season. It can be told from the corresponding call note of the Song Thrush by being more prolonged and more penetrating.

SONG THRUSH
MAR-OCT
SEP-MAR

REDWING
APR-NOV
SEP-APR

male

male

female

Blackbird

Ring Ouzel

BLACKBIRD (*Turdus merula*) (10 in.) is common in every garden, park and wood. The male is pitch black with a bright orange-yellow bill, the female is dark brown and lighter on the throat and breast. The immature birds seen in autumn show their relationship with the Thrushes by being very dark, but with rather obvious spots. Its nest is found in trees and bushes. It is often seen on lawns catching insects and worms. The song is a beautiful, mellow warbling, especially heard at dawn and at dusk.

RING OUZEL (*Turdus torquatus*) (10 in.) is a little bit smaller than the Blackbird, but otherwise black with a white crescent on upper breast. The winter plumage has light feather edges which are only really visible at close range. The female also has the white crescent, but it is not as big and the general plumage is more brownish. The juvenile birds are even more spotted than the Blackbird juveniles and lack the white crescent. It is usually found breeding in mountainous areas, but on migration it shows a preference for fields, openings bordered by hedges and woods. The song is not as full and as varied as that of the Blackbird.

BLACKBIRD

RING OUZEL   APR-OCT

SEP-MAY

ROCK THRUSH *(Monticola saxatilis)* (8 in.) is blue, red and white, the female barred brown with a red tail. It is a summer visitor to the mountainous regions in the Mediterranean area and Southern Russia.

BLUE ROCK THRUSH *(Monticola solitarius)* (8 in.) is all blue, the female bluish brown with bars. It is resident in lower mountains along the Mediterranean.

WHEATEAR *(Oenanthe oenanthe)* (6 in.) has a grey back, white rump and buffish underside, the male with a conspicuous black mask and black wings. It breeds in open moors and hill pasture, usually placing its nest among stones or in a crevice.

BLACK-EARED WHEATEAR *(Oenanthe hispanica)* (6 in.) males occur in two forms, one with buffish crown and black throat, and one with greyish crown and white throat. Females are similar to female Wheatear, but have more white on tail and lighter under-side. It is a summer visitor to dry and rocky areas along the Mediterranean.

BLACK WHEATEAR *(Oenanthe leucura)* (7 in.) has a characteristic black and white pattern. The female is similar to the male, only slightly duller in colours. It is a resident of the Iberian Peninsula, Southern France, Sardinia and Sicily.

male

female

Rock Thrush

male

Blue Rock Thrush

female   Wheatear

male

Black Wheatear

Black-eared Wheatear

WHINCHAT *(Saxicola rubetra)* (5 in.) is streaked brown above, buffish below with a very conspicuous white eye stripe and two white spots on the tail. It is found in fields with tall grass and thistles, where it nests on the ground. When perched, it sits rather upright and is constantly bobbing its tail and flicking its wings. The food consists mainly of insects, which it finds among the grass.

STONECHAT *(Saxicola torquata)* (5 in.) has black head, the male with a white half-collar brown streaked back, whitish rump and red breast. The female is duller in colour. Although it is often found in the same places as the Whinchat, it shows a preference for rougher country and occurs less commonly on cultivated ground. It is quite similar to the Whinchat in its behaviour, but, when perched, sits even more upright. Both of these closely related birds migrate mainly at night.

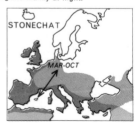

WHINCHAT
APR-OCT

STONECHAT
MAR-OCT

REDSTART (*Phoenicurus phoenicurus*) (6 in.) male has a grey back, nape and cap, rusty tail and breast, black throat and a white forehead. The female is light brown with a rusty tail. Both this and the Black Redstart constantly flicker their tails. It nests in holes and in nest-boxes in gardens, parks and open woods. It sometimes catches insects in the air, but usually picks them off the leaves of trees.

BLACK REDSTART (*Phoenicurus ochruros*) (6 in.) is mostly blackish with a red tail. The male has a white patch on the wing, conspicuous in flight. The female can be told from the female Redstart by having grey not buffish underparts. In behaviour it closely resembles the Redstart, but is more often seen on the ground. For breeding it prefers rocky areas and buildings. The nest is placed in a crevice or in a hole in a wall.

juv.

Nightingale

Thrush Nightingale

NIGHTINGALE (*Luscinia mega-rhynchos*) (7 in.) is brown above with a reddish-brown tail and buffish below. It lives from insects taken on the ground or in low bushes, where it also nests. It prefers thickets near water. Its famous song is very loud and musical. It is usually given from a hidden perch in a low bush. Although it sings all day and night during the spring, it is most often heard at dusk.

THRUSH NIGHTINGALE (*luscinia luscinia*) (7 in.) is similar in appearance, but has faint bars on the sides of breast. The song is different in having characteristic deep, bubbling notes. The relationship of these two species to the Thrushes is evident by the barred and spotted plumage of the juvenile birds. Although obviously closely related, the two species do not hybridise. In behaviour, habitat and food they are similar.

NIGHTINGALE

APR-SEP

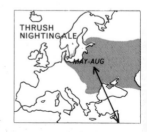

THRUSH NIGHTINGALE

MAY-AUG

Bluethroat

Robin

juv

BLUETHROAT *(Cyanosylvia svecica)* (6 in.) male in spring has a blue throat bordered with black and red, with a red or white central spot. Females are duller in colour with a dark breast band corresponding to the black bordering of the male's patch. In winter males are quite similar to females. The conspicuous red bordering of the tail is a characteristic and very good field mark. It is usually found in wet bushy areas in mountains. It has a very musical and varied song.

ROBIN *(Erithacus rubecula)* (6 in.) is brown above, has a whitish belly and a red breast and throat. Juvenile birds are very speckled and lack the red breast. It is found in gardens, parks and woods where it finds its food (insects) on the ground. It is often very tame and visits bird tables where it prefers suet. The nest is usually placed in holes with large openings on or near the ground.

BLUETHROAT

APR-SEP

ROBIN

APR-NOV

WARBLERS (Sylviinae) are small, active birds living on insects. Only a few have distinct characteristics except for the song, which is often very beautiful and at most times diagnostic. They are more often heard than seen. They are almost all migratory.

Grasshopper Warbler

Cetti's Warbler

Savi's Warbler

GRASSHOPPER WARBLER (*Locustella naevia*) (5 in.) is streaked greenish-brown above, whitish below. It nests in thick undergrowth in open country. The song is very much like the the song of a grasshopper. It is secretive in its habits.

SAVI'S WARBLER (*Locustella luscinoides*) (6 in.) is brown above, buffish below with a long, broad tail. It nests in reeds. The song is grasshopper-like but lower in tone and briefer in duration. In looks it is almost identical to the Reed Warbler, so the best identification is the song.

RIVER WARBLER (*Locustella fluviatilis*) (5 in.) is olive green above with a slightly streaked breast. It is found in wet thickets in Eastern Europe.

CETTI'S WARBLER (*Cettia cetti*) (6 in.) is dark brown above, buffish below. It breeds along the Mediterranean in tangled vegetation near water. The song is a loud repeated "tjewee".

GRASSHOPPER WARBLER

APR-SEP

SAVI'S WARBLER

APR-SEP

SEDGE WARBLER *(Acrocephalus schoenobaenus)* (5 in.) is streaked above, with a distinct white stripe over the eye. It nests in vegetation near water. The song is varied, with several harsh notes. It is sometimes given in flight.

MOUSTACHED WARBLER *(Lusciniola melanopogon)* (5 in.) is similar, but has darker brown and more reddish back. The song is melodious with a tendency to repeat each phrase several times. Its "loo-loo-loo" note distinguishes it from the Reed Warbler. It is resident in swamps along the Mediterranean.

AQUATIC WARBLER *(Acrocephalus paludicola)* (5 in.) is paler than the Sedge Warbler and has a distinct central white stripe on head. The song resembles that of the Sedge Warbler. It is a summer visitor to Italy, Northern Germany and Central Russia.

GREAT REED WARBLER *(Acrocephalus arundinaceus)* (8 in.) is uniform brown above, with an indistinct white eye stripe. The song is very loud with many harsh notes. It is found in reeds in Continental Europe, south of Scandinavia.

REED WARBLER *(Acrocephalus scirpaceus)* (5 in.) is very similar in colour. It nests in reeds all over Europe, south of Scotland and Southern Scandinavia. The song is melodious with each phrase repeated several times.

MARSH WARBLER *(Acrocephalus palustris)* (5 in.) is similar to the Reed Warbler but has light coloured legs and a more musical and varied song. It nests in open, wet areas with thick vegetation. It is a summer visitor to most of Europe north of the Mediterranean countries.

Sedge Warbler

Great Reed Warbler

Reed Warbler

Marsh Warbler

SEDGE WARBLER

APR-SEP

Icterine Warbler

Olive-tree Warbler

Olivaceous Warbler

Melodious Warbler

ICTERINE WARBLER (*Hippolais icterina*) (6 in.) is greenish-brown above, yellow below. It is a nervous and very active bird with a habit of raising its crown feathers when excited. The song is varied and very musical, with many discordant notes.

It breeds in open woods, parks and gardens where it will sing from an exposed perch.

MELODIOUS WARBLER (*Hippolais polyglotta*) (5 in.) is identical, except for the song which is faster and more babbling. Notice the difference in range of the two species.

OLIVE-TREE WARBLER (*Hippolais olivetorum*) (6 in.) has a greyish-brown upper side, whitish underside. It is found in olive groves and old oak woods of the Balkan countries.

OLIVACEOUS WARBLER (*Hippolais pallida*) (5 in.) has a pale greenish-brown upper side and white underside. In habits it is quite similar to the Icterine Warbler. It is found in gardens and parks of Southern Spain and the Balkans.

MELODIOUS AND ICTERINE WARBLERS

ICTERINE

MAY-AUG

APR-SEP

MELODIOUS

BLACKCAP *(Sylvia atricapilla)* (6 in.) is grey, darker above, lighter below, with a black cap in the male, brown in the female. It nests in gardens and open woods with undergrowth. The song is a rich Thrush-like warbling.

BARRED WARBLER *(Sylvia nisoria)* (6 in.) has characteristically barred underparts. The immature is very similar to Garden Warbler with only faint bars. It nests in thorny thickets and is a summer visitor to Eastern Europe, north to the Baltic.

GARDEN WARBLER *(Sylvia borin)* (6 in.) is greyish-brown above, buffish below. It nests in gardens and open woods with thick undergrowth. The song is a mellow warble sustained for a long time.

female

Blackcap male

im.

Barred Warbler

Garden Warbler

Orphean Warbler

It nests commonly in open gardens and farmland with bushes and brambles. The song is a fast chatter and is sometimes given in a characteristic song flight, during which the bird only rises a few yards above the bushes.

LESSER WHITETHROAT (*Sylvia curruca*) (5 in.) is very similar but is smaller and more grey on back and wings. It nests in gardens, open woods and thick hedges. The song is a low warbling ending in a harsh rattle.

ORPHEAN WARBLER (*Sylvia hortensis*) (6 in.) is greyish-brown above, whitish below and has a conspicuous white eye. It is a summer visitor to the Mediterranean countries where it nests in gardens and woods with thick undergrowth. The song is mellow and Thrush-like.

WHITETHROAT (*Sylvia communis*) (6 in.) has a brown back and wings, grey head and tail, pure white throat and a buffish-white underside.

Whitethroat

Lesser Whitethroat

WHITETHROAT

APR-SEP

LESSER WHITETHROAT

APR-OCT

DARTFORD WARBLER (*Sylvia undata*) (5 in.) has a very dark upperside and dark red underside. It has a habit of bobbing its tail up and down. It nests in low scrub in southern England, western and southern France, the Iberian Peninsula and Southern Italy.

SARDINIAN WARBLER (*Sylvia melanocephala*) (5 in.) male has a conspicuous large black cap. The female is much more brown. It nests in dry thickets along the Mediterranean, where it also winters.

SUBALPINE WARBLER (*Sylvia cantillans*) (5 in.) male has dark grey upper side and orange coloured throat and breast. The female is paler. It nests in bushes and in open woodland and is a summer visitor to the Mediterranean countries.

SPECTACLED WARBLER (*Sylvia conspicillata*) (5 in.) looks like a small Whitethroat. The song is also Whitethroat-like but shorter and not as loud. It is a summer visitor to the Western Mediterranean countries, where it nests in bushes.

FANTAILED WARBLER (*Cisticola juncidis*) (4 in.) is the smallest European Warbler. It has a very short tail. The upper part is striped brown, underside buffish. It has a characteristic display flight but is otherwise secretive in its habits. It nests in marshes and grasslands in the Mediterranean countries, where it is resident.

Dartford Warbler

Sardinian Warbler

Subalpine Warbler

Spectacled Warbler

Fantailed Warbler

Chiffchaff

Willow Warbler

Greenish Warbler

WILLOW WARBLER *(Phylloscopus trochilus)* (4 in.) is greenish above, yellowish white below with pale legs. It nests in woods, gardens, bushland and parks where it is abundant in summer. The song is a liquid, beautiful warble rising in strength and then descending. It is restless in behaviour, constantly darting around in the foliage, often flicking wings and tail.

CHIFFCHAFF *(Phylloscopus collybita)* (4 in.) is similar but a little darker and more greenish below and has dark legs. It nests in woods. The song is a very characteristic repeated "chiffchaff, chiffchaff". It is more of a woodland species than the Willow Warbler.

GREENISH WARBLER *(Phylloscopus trochiloides)* (4 in.) is almost identical to the Chiffchaff but has a wing bar and slightly more pronounced eye stripe. The song is

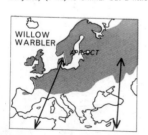

WILLOW WARBLER
APR-OCT

CHIFFCHAFF
APR-NOV
OCT-APR

Bonelli's Warbler

Wood Warbler

characteristically short and loud. It is a summer visitor to North-eastern Europe along the southern part of the Baltic Sea.

WOOD WARBLER (*Phylloscopus sibilatrix*) (5 in.) is greenish above with a yellow wing patch, yellow on throat and upper breast, white on the rest of the underside. It is found in woods, mainly deciduous, usually high in the foliage although it nests on the ground. The song is

a rather high pitched warble ending in a very fast trill.

BONELLI'S WARBLER (*Phylloscopus bonelli*) (5 in.) is grey above except for a yellow rump which is diagnostic, and small yellow patches on the wings. The underside is white. It breeds in woods with dense foliage. The nest is situated on the ground, the bird usually moving around in the trees. The song is a deliberate trill.

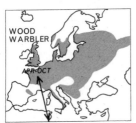

WOOD WARBLER

APR-OCT

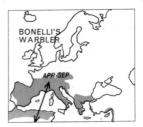

BONELLI'S WARBLER

APR-SEP

KINGLETS (*Regulidae*) are very small green birds, usually very active. The nest is globular, usually made of moss and hangs from a branch.

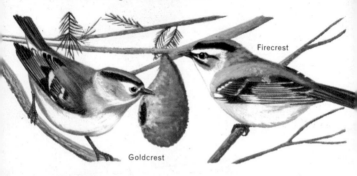

Firecrest

Goldcrest

GOLDCREST (*Regulus regulus*) (3¼ in.) is olive on back, wings and tail with two white wing bars, buffish green below and a characteristic red, yellow and black crown. It is usually found in coniferous woods, in winter in small flocks. The call is a very high-pitched repeated "zee".

FIRECREST (*Regulus ignicapillus*) (3¼ in.) is similar but has black stripe through the eye with a white stripe above. The call is lower pitched. It is found in both coniferous and deciduous woods. Its behaviour is very similar to that of the Goldcrest.

GOLDCREST

FIRECREST

MAR-OCT

FLYCATCHERS are small birds with pointed bills. They live from insects caught in the air. They sit erect on perch, waiting for an insect to fly by when they throw themselves into the air, catching the prey in the bill. They are found along margins of woods and in gardens and parks.

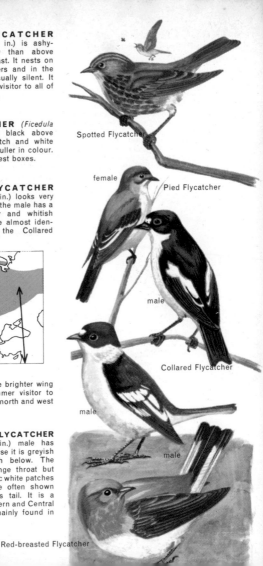

SPOTTED FLYCATCHER (*Muscicapa striata*) (6 in.) is ashy-brown, lighter below than above and with streaked breast. It nests on ledges, behind creepers and in the bark of trees. It is usually silent. It is a common summer visitor to all of Europe except Iceland.

Spotted Flycatcher

PIED FLYCATCHER (*Ficedula hypoleuca*) (5 in.) is black above with a white wing patch and white below. The female is duller in colour. It nests in holes and nest boxes.

female

Pied Flycatcher

COLLARED FLYCATCHER (*Ficedula albicollis*) (5 in.) looks very much like the Pied but the male has a complete white collar and whitish rump. The females are almost identical but those of the Collared

male

male

Collared Flycatcher

PIED FLYCATCHER

APR-SEP

Flycatcher usually have brighter wing markings. It is a summer visitor to south-eastern Europe, north and west to Germany.

male

RED-BREASTED FLYCATCHER (*Ficedula parva*) (4½ in.) male has orange throat. Otherwise it is greyish brown above, whitish below. The female lacks the orange throat but both have characteristic white patches on the tail, which are often shown as the bird cocks its tail. It is a summer visitor to Eastern and Central Europe, where it is mainly found in deciduous forests.

Red-breasted Flycatcher

ACCENTORS are Warbler-like small birds with Sparrow-like behaviour and movements. The songs are pleasant.

DUNNOCK (*Prunella modularis*) (6 in.) has a streaked brown back and wings, dark grey head and breast and white belly and streaked flanks. It nests in bushes in gardens, parks and woods. It usually seeks its food, which consists of insects, on the ground. The song is a weak, rather high-pitched warble usually given from an elevated perch. It sings almost all year round, a characteristic only

Alpine Accentor

Dunnock

shared with a few other birds, notably the Robin.

ALPINE ACCENTOR (*Prunella collaris*) (7 in.) is similar but has greyer back, chestnut spots on flanks and white throat with numerous black spots. It is found on rather bare high mountain slopes where it nests in holes. In winter it moves down to lower altitudes. The song is pleasant and often given from a rock or in display flight.

DUNNOCK
APR-OCT
OCT-APR

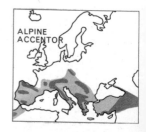

ALPINE ACCENTOR

PIPITS are small, brown streaked birds with rather long tails. They nest on the ground. Outside the breeding season they are often seen in loose flocks.

WAGTAILS are more brightly coloured but otherwise show many features in common with Pipits.

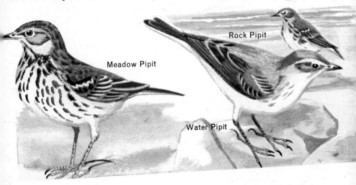

Rock Pipit

Meadow Pipit

Water Pipit

MEADOW PIPIT (*Anthus pratensis*) (6 in.) is streaked greyish brown above and streaked buffish white below. The hind claw is very long. It is found in open fields, meadows, moors, heaths and on the seashore. The call is a high-pitched "zeet", the song given in flight a musical high-pitched trill.

ROCK PIPIT (*Anthus spinoletta*) (6 in.) is similar but slightly larger and darker with dark legs. The sub-species breeding in the mountainous regions is called Water Pipit. This sub-species has a characteristic summer plumage with a pinkish breast. In winter both species are similar in plumage except that the Rock Pipit has greyish outer tail feathers. Outside the breeding season they are found on marshes and on sea coasts.

winter

summer

Red-throated Pipit

TREE PIPIT *(Anthus trivialis)* (6 in.) looks very much like the Meadow Pipit but is more yellow-brown, especially on the breast, and has a shorter hind toe. It nests in open woods and on heaths with bushes. The call is a vibrating "twe-zee"; the song is musical with many trills and is delivered in flight as the bird descends.

RED-THROATED PIPIT *(Anthus cervinus)* (6 in.) in summer has rusty throat and breast. In winter it is best told from the other Pipits by its call note which is more hoarse than that of the Meadow Pipit.

Tawny Pipit

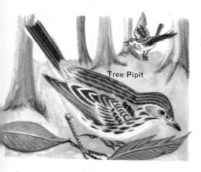

Tree Pipit

TAWNY PIPIT *(Anthus campestris)* (7 in.) is less streaked on the back than other Pipits and has a sandy coloured breast without streaks. The call note is louder than that of the Meadow Pipit. It nests on the ground in sandy areas, often along coasts in winter and on migration is also found in fields.

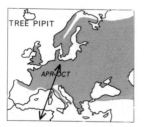

TREE PIPIT

APR-OCT

TAWNY PIPIT

OCT-APR

WHITE WAGTAIL *(Motacilla alba)* (7 in.) has a grey back, black nape, crown, throat and breast, and white face and underside. In winter the throat is white. It is found in open land, often near farms, in villages and towns. Like other Wagtails, it is constantly bobbing its long tail when walking. The British sub-species is called Pied Wagtail, and differs in having a black back.

WHITE WAGTAIL

MAR–OCT

White Wagtail

GREY WAGTAIL *(Motacilla cinerea)* (7 in.) is grey above with an eye stripe, yellow below, the male having black and the female a white throat. In summer it is always found along streams, in winter anywhere near water.

GREY WAGTAIL

Grey Wagtail

YELLOW WAGTAIL *(Motacilla flava)* (7 in.) has a green back and wings, yellow underside. The British sub-species, also found on the Continental shores adjacent to Britain, has a yellow-green head, while the continental sub-species have grey, bluish and black heads. It is found on open, wet fields and marshes. On migration it is often seen in loose flocks. It is a summer visitor to all of Europe except Iceland, Ireland and Northern Scotland.

Yellow Wagtail

WAXWINGS are medium-sized, short-tailed birds with crests. The secondaries have scarlet waxy tips. Only one species is found in Europe.

WAXWING (*Bombycilla garrulus*) (7 in.) is usually seen in flocks in winter, the numbers varying from year to year. In flight they resemble Starlings. The call is a characteristic high trill. They are seen in hedges and bushes with berries.

Waxwing

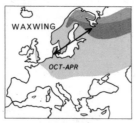

WAXWING

OCT-APR

SHRIKES (*Laniidae*) are medium-sized, long-tailed perching birds with a large head and rather strong hooked bill. They live from insects and sometimes birds caught in the air or on the ground. They sit erect when perching. The sexes are generally alike.

GREAT GREY SHRIKE (*Lanius excubitor*) (10 in.) is grey above except for black wings and tail marked with white, white below with a conspicuous broad black stripe through the eye. It is found in open country with trees and bushes and in wood margins.

Great Grey Shrike

GREAT GREY SHRIKE

APR-OCT

female

male

male

female

Woodchat Shrike

Red-backed Shrike

Lesser Grey Shrike

LESSER GREY SHRIKE *(Lanius minor)* (8 in.) is similar to the Grey Shrike but the black eye stripe extends over the front of the head and the bird is considerably smaller. It is found in the same places as the Great Grey Shrike.

RED-BACKED SHRIKE *(Lanius collurio)* (7 in.) has a chestnut back and wings, grey head and rump, a black stripe through the eye and a buffish white underside. The female is brown above, buffish white with

bars on the underside. It is found in areas with bushes where it nests, usually in a thorny bush. As other Shrikes, it will spear its prey on a thorn.

WOODCHAT SHRIKE *(Lanius senator)* (7 in.) is buffish white below, black above with chestnut nape, white rump and two white patches on each wing. The immature is brown barred with two light patches on the wing. It is found in open, dry country with bushes and trees.

STARLINGS are medium sized birds with short round tails and rather long bills. They are often seen in large flocks and often seen feeding on the ground.

Starling

SPOTLESS STARLING (*Sturnus unicolor*) (9 in.) is similar but never has any spots. It is found on the Iberian Peninsula and the islands of the Western Mediterranean where it is resident.

Spotless Starling

STARLING (*Sturnus vulgaris*) (9 in.) is glossy black with light coloured spots in winter, solid black with a metallic green and purple gloss in summer with only a few specks on the back. It has a long, straight bill which is bright yellow in summer. The immatures are light brown with a whitish throat. It lives on insects and berries etc., and nests in holes in trees and houses and also in nest boxes. It is one of the best known birds.

ROSE-COLOURED STARLING (*Sturnus roseus*) (9 in.) is black with a rosy back and belly; the immatures are more faintly coloured. It is found in south-eastern Europe but at intervals birds penetrate to more western countries.

Rose-coloured Starling

STARLING

MAR-NOV

FINCHES AND BUNTINGS form a rather heterogenous group of seed-eating birds. The bill is characteristically short and strong. They are medium sized to small and the sexes are usually different in plumage. Many have beautiful songs and characteristic call notes.

Bullfinch

male

female

Hawfinch

The call note is a loud "cik". It is wary and not often seen.

HAWFINCH (*Coccothraustes coccothraustes*) (7 in.) is brown with a grey nape, white and black wings, black throat and a very large bill. It is found in mature deciduous woods where it nests in the tree tops. It feeds on fruit, nuts and seeds. It is usually seen singly but in winter sometimes in small flocks.

BULLFINCH (*Pyrrhula pyrrhula*) (6 in.) has a black cap, wings and tail, grey back, white rump and red breast and belly. The female has buffish brown underside, the bill is short and thick. It is found in gardens, parks and woods, in winter in flocks. The voice is a soft, plaintive whistle. The song is a beautiful low warbling. When feeding in trees and bushes they move about in a rather leisurely manner.

Goldfinch

juv.

Greenfinch

female

GREENFINCH (*Carduelis chloris*) (6 in.) is green with yellow patches on wings and tail. The female is brownish-green. It has a display flight where the wing beats are very slow and deliberate and the wings held with tips pointing upward. The song is canary-like, the call is short, trilled. It is found in gardens, parks and open woods where it usually nests in bushes. As is the case with many of its relatives, it feeds its young with insects.

GOLDFINCH (*Carduelis carduelis*) (5 in.) has a black nape, tail and wing, (the latter with broad yellow stripe), brown back and breast, white belly, cheeks and rump and a bright red face. It nests in open gardens, parks, fields and meadows where it is usually seen in pairs or small groups (families). It lives on seeds taken from the ground or off the plant. It is particularly fond of thistles. The call is a characteristic "switt-witt-witt-witt". Because of its bright colours and Canary-like song, it is often kept as a cage bird.

GREENFINCH

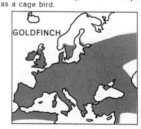

GOLDFINCH

flanks and dark wings and tail. The yellow rump is very distinctive in flight. It is found in gardens, parks and open woods. The song, sometimes given in flight, is Canary-like with hissing notes interspersed.

CITRIL FINCH *(Serinus citrinella)* (5 in.) is greenish with grey nape and two wing bars. It nests in coniferous forests in the Alps, northeastern Spain, Sardinia and Corsica.

SISKIN *(Carduelis spinus)* (5 in.) is green with streaked back and flanks, yellow breast and eye stripe, black cap and throat and yellow patches on tail and wings. It nests in coniferous forests but is also seen in birch and alders, particularly in flocks during winter. Its call note is a characteristic two-tone squeak.

SERIN *(Serinus serinus)* (4½ in.) is yellow with streaked back, head and

SERIN

MAR-NOV

SISKIN

SEP-APR

Citril Finch

147

female male

Twite

Linnet

LINNET (*Acanthis cannabina*) (5 in.) has a brown back, grey head and buffish underside with a rosy forehead and breast. There is a white patch on the wing which is easily seen in flight. It nests in gardens, parks, heaths and open country with bushes and trees. The song, usually given from a perch, is a pleasant twitter. In winter it is often seen in flocks.

TWITE
OCT-APR

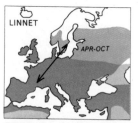

LINNET
APR-OCT

TWITE (*Acanthis flavirostris*) (5 in.) is streaked brown with a pink rump. It has a yellow bill which distinguishes it from the Linnet in winter plumage. It nests on moors. In winter it is seen in flocks on open fields, marshes and meadows. The flight call has a distinctive nasal quality. It is very noisy, twittering whilst in flight.

REDPOLL (*Acanthis flammea*) (5 in.) is streaked grey and white with red forehead and the males with rosy breasts. The flight is undulating. It is usually seen in flocks. It nests in Iceland, the British Isles, Northern Scandinavia, Central Russia and the Alps, scattering over larger parts of Northern Europe in winter.

Redpoll

CROSSBILL *(Loxia curvirostra)* male (7 in.) is red with black wings and tail. The female is greenish, the immature greyish green. The tips of the lower and upper mandibles cross each other. This peculiar shape is advantageous as the bird can reach the seeds hidden in the cones of conifers. It is always seen in or close to coniferous forests. It can breed in all seasons. In years when the production of conifer seed is low the Crossbill will wander in large flocks and can be found all over Europe.

PARROT CROSSBILL *(Loxia pytyopsittacus)* (7 in.) is similar to the Crossbill but has larger bill. It is mainly seen in pines whereas the

CROSSBILL

Crossbill prefers spruce. It breeds in North-eastern Europe, in winter reaching west to Denmark, Germany and Austria.

TWO-BARRED CROSSBILL *(Loxia leucoptera)* (6 in.) has a much weaker bill than the two preceeding species to which it is similar except for two white wing bars. It is found mainly in larch woods. It breeds in North-eastern Europe, wintering around the Baltic, and occasionally further south and west.

Crossbill

female

im.

male

Parrot Crossbill

male

female

Two-barred Crossbill

CHAFFINCH (*Fringilla coelebs*) male (6 in.) has reddish underside, blue crown and nape, chestnut back, two white wing bars and a black tail bordered with white. The female is olive green but with the same white areas as the male. It is very common in woods, parks and gardens. In winter it is seen in flocks, sometimes numbering thousands of birds. The song is short, loud and pleasant. It is one of the most common European birds.

BRAMBLING(*Fringilla montifringilla*) (6 in.) male has black head and back, orange breast and forewing and white belly and rump. In winter the black areas are barred dark brown. The female is much duller in coloration but the white rump is very distinctive, particularly in flight. It is seen in open fields and deciduous woods in large flocks in winter, in woods in summer. The flocks often mix with Chaffinches. The flight call has a nasal quality.

female

male

male

Cirl Bunting

female

Yellowhammer

YELLOWHAMMER (*Emberiza citrinella*) (7 in.) has a yellow head and underside and an orange brown rump. It is seen on open fields and meadows, often perched on a pole or wire. The song is a characteristic and resembles "little-bit-of-bread-and-no-cheese". The female is more dull in coloration than the male. In winter it is often seen in small flocks, sometimes mixing with other birds like Chaffinches or Bramblings.

CIRL BUNTING (*Emberiza cirlus*) (7 in.) is yellow with a characteristic black and grey pattern on head. The female is very similar to female Yellowhammer but has greenish brown rump. It is found in open country with bushes, trees and hedgerows and is often seen in winter in mixed flocks with Yellowhammers. The song is a monotonous repitition of one note.

YELLOW-HAMMER

CIRL BUNTING

Corn Bunting male

male

Ortolan Bunting

female

female

CORN BUNTING (*Emberiza*) *calandra*) (7 in.) is streaked brown. It is very chunky with a thick bill. It nests in open fields. The song, which is often given from a perch on a pole or wire, is a metallic, rapid jingle. The male is polygamous, often covering a very large territory where his females build their nests.

ORTOLAN BUNTING (*Emberiza hortulana*) (7 in.) has a greenish grey head and breast with a yellow throat. The back is brown with streaks, the belly orange brown. The song is like the Yellowhammer's but slower and more varied. It nests in gardens, parks and open country with bushes and thickets. In autumn, Ortolans become very fat and many are caught in traps, their meat being regarded by many as a great delicacy.

CORN BUNTING

ORTOLAN BUNTING

APR-SEP

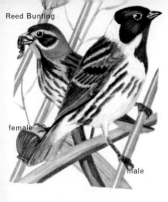

Reed Bunting

female

male

a perch on a reed. It is usually found alone or in small scattered groups of its own species.

ROCK BUNTING (*Emberiza cia*) (6 in.) has a pale grey head and neck with black facial lines, orange brown belly and rump and a streaked brown back. It often flicks its tail, showing the white markings. It is found in rocky areas but is not restricted to bare rock country as it can often be found close to, or in, trees. The song is short and high-pitched.

ROCK
BUNTING

REED BUNTING (*Emberiza schoeniclus*) (6 in.) has a brown streaked back, white belly and hind neck and a pitch black head, throat and breast. The female lacks the black colours. It is common in swamps, marshes and shores with reeds in which it nests. The song, ascending in speeds, is rather high-pitched and is often delivered from

REED
BUNTING

APR-OCT

male

winter

summer

male

Lapland Bunting

LAPLAND BUNTING (*Calcarius lapponicus*) (6 in.) male is characteristically coloured black, white and chestnut in summer. The female and the winter plumage is plainer, being striped with a rusty coloured nape. It nests in northern-most Scandinavia and Russia, wintering along the North Sea where it is usually seen in fields and on shores.

Rock Bunting

male

male
winter

Snow Bunting

summer

male

SNOW FINCH (*Montifringilla nivalis*) (7 in.) is grey with large white patches on the wings and tail, a brown back and black throat. It often jerks its tail. In flight it looks more white than when perched. It sits rather upright, giving it a characteristic silhouette. It nests in high mountains, usually above 6,000 ft. It sings from a perch or in display flight and the voice is rather high-pitched.

SNOW FINCH

SNOW BUNTING (*Plectrophenax nivalis*) (7 in.) is white with black wing tips and centre part of tail, a brown back and crown. The female is darker and more brownish. It nests on bare mountains in the far north, often close to houses. In winter it is seen in flocks along seashores and on open fields and marshes. The flight is characteristic and has been described as "dancing". In summer the male's plumage is extremely beautiful and is more black than in the winter plumage.

Snow Finch

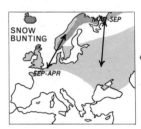

SNOW BUNTING

MAR-SEP

SEP-APR

Spanish Sparrow

male

Tree Sparrow

male

male

House Sparrow

female

HOUSE SPARROW (Passer domesticus) (6 in.) is known by everyone. It is common in all cities and around every farm where it nests in colonies within roofs and in haystacks. Sometimes it will build a big cone-shaped nest in bushes or ivy. It can breed all year round, but seldom does so in winter. It lives mainly on seeds and bread-crumbs, etc., but can take insects.

SPANISH SPARROW (Passer hispaniolensis) (6 in.) is similar to the House Sparrow but has a chestnut crown and more extensive black on the breast. The female is identical to female House Sparrow. It is found in the southern part of the Mediterranean countries.

TREE SPARROW (Passer montanus) (5½ in.) has a more delicate build, a chestnut, not grey, crown and a smaller black area. It breeds in woods, parks and gardens and is not associated with humans like the House Sparrow. The nest is made in holes in trees, nest boxes and sometimes in haystacks with House Sparrows.

TREE SPARROW

ROCK SPARROW (Petronia petronia) (6 in.) looks like a female House Sparrow but has a striped crown, a yellow spot on the breast and white spots on the tip of the tail. It is found on the slopes of the Pyrenees and elsewhere in France, Spain, Italy and Greece and the Mediterranean Islands.

HOUSE SPARROW

Rock Sparrow

INDEX